Doing Business in Russia

Doing Business in Russia

A Concise Guide

Volume I

Anatoly Zhuplev

BEP BUSINESS EXPERT PRESS

Doing Business in Russia: A Concise Guide, Volume I

First published in 2017 by
Business Expert Press, LLC
222 East 46th Street, New York, NY 10017
www.businessexpertpress.com

ISBN-13: 978-1-63157-128-2 (paperback)
ISBN-13: 978-1-63742-336-3 (hardcover)
ISBN-13: 978-1-63157-129-9 (e-book)

Business Expert Press International Business Collection

Collection ISSN: 1948-2752 (print)
Collection ISSN: 1948-2760 (electronic)

Cover and interior design by Exeter Premedia Services Private Ltd., Chennai, India

First edition: 2017

10 9 8 7 6 5 4 3 2 1

Abstract

Russia is the world's largest geographic area, major economy, and important power in the global political-economic landscape. Over the past quarter century, following the landmark dissolution of the U.S.S.R., Russia has become a premier global marketplace despite remaining enigmatic and challenging. The book strives to serve as a concise guide in understanding Russia from an international business perspective.

You will learn about strategic issues, business drivers, pros, cons, costs, and risks of international expansion. The coverage includes analytical tools, practical applications, sources of information, and assistance in international business research. These are followed by Russia's macroeconomic profile, drivers, strategic strengths and weaknesses in the comparative global context, including its international market attractiveness and primary opportunities for U.S. companies.

The book examines Russia's main industries, their profiles, dynamics and business attractiveness, consumer trends, and marketing strategies. The discussion of Russia's regions covers regional subdivisions and economic profiles with the focus on the city of Moscow commanding top attractiveness from the domestic and international business perspective. The book covers the drivers and trends of the Russian small business sector and entrepreneurial business venturing.

Despite the onslaught of capitalism and globalization, Russia retains its relationship-driven culture. The book provides insights in Russian culture by evaluating the determinants of Russian culture, its national profile in major global cross-cultural studies, and practical cultural applications in business, negotiations, and communications.

The book's pedagogy includes critical information sources and skill development exercises and cases on doing business in Russia.

Keywords

business, commerce, culture, entrepreneurship, industries, international, Moscow, regions, Russia, strategy, trade

Contents

Acknowledgments

The author would like to acknowledge the help of all the people involved in this project and, particularly, express appreciation to the colleagues at Loyola Marymount University and Business Expert Press for outstanding editorial support.

Anatoly Zhuplev
Loyola Marymount University, U.S.A.

Introduction

Russia is the world's largest geographic area, a BRIC economy, and an important player in the global landscape. Over the past quarter century, following the dissolution of the Soviet Union, Russia has become a magnet for international commerce, trade, and foreign investment. Its post-Soviet development has been marked by profound changes in the nation's political-economic conditions and business environment, improving Russia's business climate and transforming the nation into a more attractive marketplace. Despite improvements, this progress has been uneven and sporadic. In many ways, Russia remains an enigmatic and challenging place for doing business.

Apart from general difficulties in starting and managing international business ventures common for many countries worldwide, obstacles specific to doing business in Russia often stem from its unique features: enormous geographic size, harsh climate, remarkable regional variations, and remote regional location relative to major global markets. Over the centuries Russia has been governed under a highly centralized political-economic system causing inefficiencies and instability, particularly acute during periods of power transition. Its extraordinary dependence on the energy sector in domestic and foreign policy generates waves of economic booms and busts as global oil and natural gas prices tend to skyrocket and plunge in cycles. Russia's foreign policy, buttressed by its dominant regional role and status as a major military power, and yet constrained by limited global business competitiveness, is closely intertwined with the dynamics in the energy-dependent domestic economy. Russia is also noticeably different in cultural values, norms, and attitudes from its neighbors in the Eurasian region—both near and far. Understanding these cultural differences in a relationship-oriented country like Russia is critical for business communications, marketing, negotiations, management, and overall success in business endeavors.

This book, designed as a brief business guide on Russia, is written from an international business perspective. It first examines strategic issues, business drivers, benefits, costs, and risks associated with international expansion in a general context. The book also offers a number of analytical tools, practical applications, references to information databases, and sources of consulting assistance in international business research that are instrumental in the Russian context. Major business concepts, frameworks, and extensive factual material related to doing business in Russia are integrated throughout the book. An understanding of a country as large and intricate as Russia requires a complex, multifaceted approach. The application of this approach includes two main aspects that this book explores: the nation's sectorial/industrial picture and regional-economic composition. Under the sectorial/industrial aspect, the discussion focuses on main industries, their profiles, trends, drivers and constrains, business attractiveness, consumer trends, and applicable marketing strategies. Under the regional aspect, the book looks at Russia's regional structure, regional subdivisions, and economic profiles, with special attention given to the city of Moscow that, compared to other Russian regions, is characterized by higher attractiveness from both domestic and international business perspectives. Although the Russian economy is dominated by large companies, often fully or partially government-owned and/or controlled in certain ways, Russia's small business sector is examined in the book as it also has its own dynamics and international business potential: the book discusses drivers and trends in the Russian small business sector and fundamentals of entrepreneurial business venturing.

As with any nation, Russia has its own unique cultural character and mindset that translate into trends, business patterns, and practices evolving over the centuries along with the ever-changing determinants of the national business environment and culture. Despite technological developments, the advent of capitalism and unfolding globalization, in many ways Russia remains a relationship-driven culture when it comes to business and politics. The book examines the Russian culture first by evaluating critical determinants of its national culture, highlighting its national profile as reflected in several recent groundbreaking global cross-cultural studies, and then drawing practical cultural implications for international business, negotiations, and communications.

Beyond the business subject matter, the book's pedagogy includes sources of business research information, skill development exercises and cases on doing business in Russia. The importance of skill development exercises and cases is twofold. First, traditional pedagogies relying on mere extraction and transmission of information, and memorization-based knowledge are becoming increasingly obsolete, static, and ineffective. Disruptive technological, product and marketing innovations, proliferation of globalization, propagation of the Internet, electronic databases, social networks, and other powerful drivers propel the role of business skills and practical applications in strategic growth and professional careers. Second, skill development is particularly important in the field of international business in emerging markets like Russia, where business environment and situations are often fluid, prone to change, and have no clear-cut solutions from general theory applications that are distilled by past and current experience.

Organization of the Book
Volume I

Chapter 1 Internationalization of the Company: Strategic Survival and Success through Competition and Growth

Main points in this chapter: Why go international? Analytical tools for international expansion: company, industry, and country research; and strategic benefits, costs, and risks of international expansion: practical applications, sources of information, and assistance.

The opening chapter discusses general issues of internationalization that a company faces as an organic part of its economic mission under the driving and constraining forces of globalization. In the strategic analysis and decision-making process, these forces take the forms of business opportunities, costs, and risks. This chapter looks at issues, steps, and analytical tools applicable in the process of international expansion of a company. It analyzes these components in terms of interconnections between international expansion and company's background, organizational culture and existing strategic mission, strengths, weaknesses, and resource availability. In examining short-term and long-term strategic benefits, costs, and risks associated with international expansion, the chapter explores how they balance against each other in an overall context. This analysis continues by rationalizing country/market selection and deciding on the best entry mode in international expansion. Further on, the discussion assesses the pros and cons of early versus late entry into an international target market and, depending on the timing decision, whether it makes sense to expand to this market on small versus large scale.

General discussion of strategic internationalization is supported by factual illustrations contrasting Russia with some comparator countries. This chapter contains an array of analytical tools, frameworks, and applications pertaining to the internationalization process.

Chapter 2 Russia: Attractiveness in a Global Perspective

Main points in this chapter: Russia's macroeconomic profile, drivers, and dynamics; strategic strengths and weaknesses in the comparative global context; market attractiveness, ease and risks of doing business; leading sectors for U.S. exports and investment.

The chapter portrays Russia's macroeconomic profile and examines its relative role in the world. This analysis is framed in a historical and comparative context contrasting Russian macroeconomic indicators with those of its three fellow BRIC countries, Brazil, China, and India as well as two "aspirational comparators," the United States and Germany.

Following this macroeconomic analysis, the chapter explores Russia's market attractiveness, ease, costs, and risks of doing business. The discussion differentiates two major cases of international business expansion that vary in their drivers and dynamics: a marketing-driven expansion and a manufacturing-driven expansion. This analysis is supported by factual information derived from authoritative reports by the World Bank, World Economic Forum, and major insurance companies with global outreach.

Drawing on the annual list of leading sectors for U.S. exports and investments in commercial sectors in the U.S. Commercial Service's Country Commercial Guide 2016 for Russia, the chapter provides a market analysis summary for one of the leading sectors, the Medical Equipment industry. Using the step-by-step export-related market research format discussed in Chapter 1, this analysis of the Russian Medical Equipment market examines the consumption and production of competitive products, ascertaining sources of competition, including the extent of domestic industry production and that of major foreign countries, analyzing factors affecting marketing and the use of products in each market, identifying local market entry barriers, and looking into price competition.

Chapter 3 Russia's Main Industries and Their Attractiveness for International Business

Main points in this chapter: Industry structure; main industries, their profiles, trends and business attractiveness; consumer trends and marketing strategies.

The chapter examines the composition of Russia's economy across its major sectors: agriculture, industry, and services. This analysis looks at the dynamics within each of these sectors and provides factual information illustrating Russia's comparative standing and attractiveness against its fellow BRIC countries and "aspirational comparators," the United States and Germany. A critical review of Russia's main industries, their profiles, and trends conveys a sense of their business attractiveness from an international investor or business person's perspective. The energy sector is given special attention in this analysis, as this sector plays a critical role in the Russian domestic economy and foreign policy as the premier hard currency earner, contributor of the lion share to the federal budget, and a powerful lever in foreign policy. The chapter discusses the state, trends, dynamics, and outlook for Russia's energy sector with an emphasis on the oil and natural gas industries. Over the past two decades, Russia's oil and gas exports, under high global demand and skyrocketing prices, have generated spectacular windfalls and propelled the nation's political-economic growth—uplifting Russia's global role as a foreign investment destination and premier market for goods and services. However, in the span of the past two to three years, significant changes in global energy supply and demand, dramatic downward trends in global oil and gas prices, the emergence of competitive sources of alternative energy, as well as negative regional and national political-economic developments involving Russia have altogether fundamentally altered the business landscape in Russia's energy sector. This chapter discusses these trends, dynamics, and changes with a view of emerging international business opportunities.

Apart from oil and gas, Russia offers high commercial potential in a range of other economic sectors and industries. The chapter discusses three examples of the market landscape reflecting best business opportunities for U.S.-based companies in Russia: Agricultural Equipment, Medical Equipment, and Cosmetics and Perfumery.

Concluding the chapter is an overview of the top five latest consumer trends in Russia: consumer confidence low as a result of economic downturn; online shopping boosted by consumers looking for lower prices; Russians increasingly adopting healthier lifestyles; older Russians delaying retirement; and high cost of mortgages keeps many off the property ladder.

Volume II

Chapter 1 Russian Regions: Business Dynamics and Attractiveness

Main points in this chapter: Russia: regional subdivisions and economic profiles; business environment in the city of Moscow: domestic and international perspective.

Regional analysis is part of strategic business research preceding a company's international strategic expansion to its target country. Regional strategy has particular meaning and importance in Russia, a large country characterized by intricate history and geography, multifaceted demographics and a complex political-economic landscape across its regions.

The chapter begins with an overview of the Russian regional amalgam, administrative subdivisions, and comparative characteristics of economic development and business attractiveness across the regions. These comparisons reveal the Central Federal District as one of the most economically attractive in the nation from an international business standpoint in both trade and investment. In particular, the city of Moscow and Moscow Oblast as part of the Central Federal District have long been national leaders in terms of their competitive standing in industry, services, trade, attracting foreign investment, education, and other areas.

Further discussion in this chapter describes the Russian Investment Agency and its role in support of international business development across the nation with a comparative analytical focus on four regions: the cities of Moscow and St. Petersburg as well as the Moscow and Leningrad regions. Further on, the chapter focuses on regional exploration of the business environment and investment potential of the city of Moscow, Russia's absolute leader. For this purpose the discussion is structured under the generalized framework used by the Moscow City Investment Agency that is part of the Federal Russian Investment Agency system. This generalized framework includes two main sections: "Investments in Moscow" and "Guide for Investor." Their intended purpose, respectively, is to highlight strategic advantages/benefits of investing or conducting business in Moscow and provide a potential investor/business operator with orientation on starting and running business. The framework also includes extensive factual information. The chapter covers Moscow's investment climate factors, investment opportunities, economic-geographical position, business activity, investment activity, conditions for investment, and urban environment.

Chapter 2 Small Business, Entrepreneurship, and Business Venturing in Russia

Main points in this chapter: Russian small business and entrepreneurship sector: origins, drivers and trends; entrepreneurial business venturing in Russia.

Russia's international trade and foreign direct investment landscapes are dominated by large corporations, some of them with global outreach. Large corporations, compared to small and medium size enterprises (SMEs), often possess competitive advantages: ample resources, global market access, greater eligibility for outside financing, more comprehensive business expertise, and cost advantages from economies of scale. This chapter argues that foreign-based SMEs contemplating expansion or already operating in Russia are not well positioned to partake in business-to-government and business-to-business commerce in Russia due to their strategic disadvantages. For example SMEs are often not capable of fulfilling sizeable orders and meeting logistical requirements needed for participation in Russian government procurement programs and big scope industrial supply chains. Nevertheless, some industries and regions in Russia present potential small business and entrepreneurship opportunities for foreign-based marketers, manufacturers and investors.

The chapter begins by discussing the origins, drivers, trends, and current profile of Russia's small business and entrepreneurship sector. This narrative is supported by a comparative analysis of the Russia's SMEs in contrast to their European counterparts. Further analysis concentrates on the sectorial/industrial composition and regional structure of Russian SMEs.

Over the years, Russia has been part of the continuous global study of entrepreneurship, "Global Entrepreneurship Monitor (GEM) 2015." Drawing on the latest annual GEM report and other recent studies of Russian SMEs, the chapter portrays Russia's comparative picture in the international context. Similar to the earlier discussion, this analysis compares and contrasts Russia's entrepreneurial dynamics with those of its fellow BRIC economies, regional peers, and "aspirational comparators."

The rest of the chapter discusses the foundations of conducting commerce and entrepreneurial ventures in the country, drawing on another annual business report, Russia's Country Commercial Guide (CCG Russia). This discussion covers topics ranging from using an agent or distributor, establishing an office, the fundamentals of corporate taxation, franchising, marketing, joint ventures, electronic commerce trade promotion, customer support, intellectual property protection, and due diligence.

Chapter 3 Russian Business Culture

Main points in this chapter: Determinants of Russian culture; Russia's national profile in major global cross-cultural studies; practical cultural applications on doing business in Russia.

The chapter begins with an exploration of Russian culture as a general framework. This general analysis is followed by a discussion of the determinants of Russian culture and cultural implications ranging from the national geographic landscape, history, demographics, national governance, religion, to the social system and family. The next section focuses on Russia's national profile as reflected in the findings from three seminal global cross-cultural studies: Hofstede's Cultural Dimensions, the GLOBE Study, and the World Values Survey. The chapter culminates in discussing practical cultural applications of doing business in Russia.

Cultural lessons and implications for international business translate into three key areas that stand out in their practical importance: international negotiations, international marketing, and international management. Discussion of Russian culture in this context is supported by empirical recommendations from survey-based research, major international cultural guides on doing business and observations based on first-hand experiences and insights from expatriates living and working in Russia.

Appendix I Information Sources on Doing Business in Russia

This supplementary section includes 54 authoritative public and commercial sources of information (databases, periodic reports, etc.) available from major global and regional institutions, national government agencies and NGOs, premier international consultancies, insurance companies and rating agencies, as well as industry-related analytical centers.

Appendix II Skill Development Exercises and Cases on Doing Business in Russia

Main points in this chapter: Learning by doing; skill development exercises; cases.

A complex, dynamic, and rapidly evolving international business landscape makes specific knowledge and information obsolete. With that, traditional pedagogies relying on mere extraction and transmission of information, and memorization-based knowledge are becoming increasingly ineffective. This elevates the importance and role of business skills and practical applications in strategic growth, decision making, professional careers, and education. Skill development is particularly important in the field of international business in emerging markets like Russia where business environment and situations are often fluid, prone to change, and have no clear-cut solutions from theory applications distilled by past and current experience.

This chapter includes 10 skill development exercises. Among them is a take-home final exam assignment: "Export-related market research in BRICS." In essence, this is a mini-feasibility study in strategic marketing that can be used either as a take-home exam or an exercise in skill development. The chapter also includes six short cases on doing business in Russia. The cases represent different industries, countries, and Russian regions.

These materials are designed as a platform to apply theoretical concepts, integrate them with factual support and empirical information on a national, regional, industry or company level, often presented in a comparative cross-country context. Integrated together in a business format, these skill development exercises and business cases intend to facilitate critical and conceptual business skill development thinking in international business research, analysis, problem solving, and decision making.

CHAPTER 1

Internationalization of the Company

Strategic Survival and Success through Competition and Growth

Capital eschews no profit, or very small profit, just as nature abhors a vacuum. With adequate profit, capital is very bold. A certain 10 percent will ensure its employment anywhere; 20 percent certain will produce eagerness; 50 percent, positive audacity; 100 percent will make it ready to trample on all human laws; 300 percent, and there is not a crime at which it will scruple, nor a risk it will not run, even to the chance of its owner being hanged.

—T.J. Dunning, l. c., pp. 35, 36.
Karl Marx Capital. Vol. 1

Main Points in This Chapter

- Why go international?
- Analytical tools for international expansion: company, industry, and country research.
- Strategic benefits, costs, and risks of international expansion: practical applications, sources of information, and assistance.

Why Go International?

Arguably, the economic mission of the corporation is to maximize its financial performance and profits.[1] Modern-day corporations have come a long
way from the times of industrial revolution so grotesquely characterized
by Karl Marx, a prominent communist thinker of the 19th century. In
pursuit of their economic mission, corporations in our time do participate
in business activities resulting in job creation, environmental protection,
support of social causes, community development, and even go as far as
corporate philanthropy. However, all things considered, the economic—
profit-making and wealth-growing—mission of the corporation remains
fundamentally paramount.

---

[1] Peter Drucker, a prominent management authority, had developed a contem-
porary concept of the corporation in the post WWII decade in his seminal book
"Concept of the Corporation" (1946). Since then, corporations have come of
their managerial age to experience many transformations. Milton Friedman, a
Nobel Laureate in economics, was a staunch proponent of the economic mission of business enterprise as its premier strategic driver: Friedman's argument
in response to his critics on the corporate social responsibility side was that ultimately the social responsibility of business is to increase its profits (Friedman
1970). Over the past two decades, sustainable development has become an
emerging corporate trend (Elkington 1997). The concept of sustainability
expands corporate mission under the "triple bottom line" framework emphasiz-
ing social and environmental priorities in addition to financial performance and
mere profit-making. The late Michael Porter of Harvard has been exploring and
advocating a corporate concept of shared value. According to Porter, the purpose
of the corporation must be redefined as creating shared value, not just profit per
se. This will drive the next wave of innovation and productivity growth in the
global economy (Porter 2011). Adding complexity are the differences between
the missions of the for-profit versus not-for-profit corporations. These streams
of thought, frameworks, and applications vary across the world: the ideas of
sustainability, corporate social responsibility, and shared values have been more
prevalent among economically advanced countries as opposed to less developed
nations. While viewing sustainable development, corporate social responsibility,
and shared values in positive light, this book focuses on economic aspects of the
corporation in the international business context.

Globalization that has intensified in the second half of the 20th century[2] vastly expands socioeconomic boundaries and development opportunities for global regions, nations, industries, business entities, entrepreneurs, and individuals. Along with providing new horizons and opportunities, globalization levels the playing field, facilitates interdependence across nations and industries, and exerts competitive pressures on all of the actors involved. These forces facilitate corporate drive toward internationalization through the creation of and the ongoing changes in the landscape of business opportunities and competitive pressures (Hill and Hult 2016). Those absent or slow in embracing this process may miss out on business opportunities or experience strategic losses in the evolving global competitive field.

Unless a corporate decision to go international is a political, personal, or emotional one, it is usually driven either by *opportunity* (the forces of strategic attraction overseas *pull* the company internationally) or by *necessity* (the forces of strategic competition or domestic government regulation *push* the company overseas). The scope and format of the corporate involvement overseas depends on many conditions stemming from the company retrospective background and current strategic position, including its internal strengths and weaknesses. It is also predetermined by the current state, drivers, and future trends in the external business environment and its market forces. From the company's strategic standpoint, these external factors and dynamics translate into business opportunities and threats. A company's retrospective background and developments determine its current business performance, profile, and strategic posture. Current dynamics constitute a foundation supporting its future dynamics, developments, and growth.

---

[2] Globalization is driven by technological advances in ocean and air transportation, communications, and political-economic liberalization resulting in falling barriers for international trade and foreign investment. De-colonization and democratization in Africa, Asia, and Latin America in the second half of the 20th century, the demise of communism and dissolution of the U.S.S.R. in the 1990s, along with their large-scale impacts on the rest of the world, have led to dramatic expansion of global commerce and opened new markets for trade and investment.

Going international exposes a company to an external political-economic environment; in a broad business sense, this environment can be strategically defined as a set of interdependent factors or variables that, taken together, comprise the Political, Economic, Social, and Technological (PEST/PESTEL/PESTLE[3]) framework. In state-controlled or mixed economies (e.g., China, Japan, or France) governments tend to impose more regulations and exercise more protectionist attitudes toward domestic consumers, producers, and economic development priorities, sometimes at the expense of foreign entities. In free market economies (e.g., Hong Kong, Singapore, Australia) with their less stringent government regulations, more efficient markets, and less "cradle-to-grave" type broad social support, the survival and success of business enterprises occur through a more or less open competition and growth taking place on a relatively free for all, even playing field.[4] A progressively competitive global business environment facilitates opportunities and at the same time creates competitive forces that companies cannot strategically ignore by standing still and clinging to the status quo; in order to stay in business and grow, they must compete or be overtaken by competition sooner or later. With that, internationalization should be viewed as an organic part of the company's development and growth, and embracing international rivalry, international strategic alliances, or engaging in other

---

[3] A PEST (political, economic, social, and technological) analysis looks at a framework of macroenvironmental factors used in the environmental scanning component of strategic management. PESTEL expands PEST in the same context by adding Environmental and Legal components.

[4] Economic classifications of the nations across the world vary. Depending on the degree of government ownership and control over the national economy as measured against private sector, in general, there are three major types of economic systems: a market economy, a command economy, and a mixed economy (Hill and Hult 2016). Sometimes, market economies are further categorized into the free market economies (e.g., the United States, Singapore) and social market economies (e.g., Germany); command economies (e.g., Cuba, North Korea) are sometimes also categorized as centrally planned, state-controlled economies; and mixed economies (e.g., Sweden, France)—can be found on a continuum between market and command economies.

pursuits should be viewed as an integral part of the company's competitive strategy.

Analytical Tools for International Expansion: Company, Industry, and Country Research

In general, strategic business research associated with international expansion involves three major aspects: company analysis, industry analysis, and country analysis.

Company Analysis

Company analysis is an important starting point that strives to identify a company's capabilities, available resources, and strategic readiness to internationalize. Prior to making an important step involving significant strategic commitments, resources, costs, and risks, it is of paramount importance to assess whether the company can survive internationalization and sustain strategic, tactical, and operational shocks associated with international expansion.

One popular tool for company analysis is the SWOT[5] framework (Figure 1.1). In a broader context, SWOT is often used in conjunction with the PEST/PESTEL framework applicable to both internal and external business environmental analysis that should precede international expansion.

Other effective and easy-to-use export-related diagnostic frameworks are the Export Readiness Assessment Tool[6] (International Trade Compliance Institute 2016), the questionnaire "Are You Export Ready?"

---

[5] A SWOT analysis is a strategic analytical method designed to evaluate the Strengths, Weaknesses, Opportunities, and Threats involved in a project, a business venture, or a business enterprise. It involves identification of the objectives of the business enterprise and ascertaining the internal and external factors that are favorable and unfavorable toward achieving these objectives.

[6] The Export Readiness Assessment developed by Maurice Kogon determines a company's export readiness by its answers to 23 questions about its present operations, attitudes, and products.

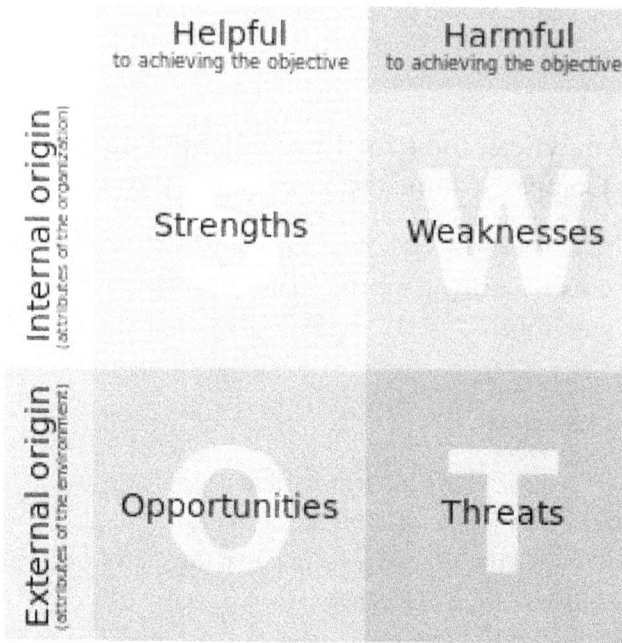

Figure 1.1 SWOT framework

(https://new.export.gov/2016), and the CORE Diagnostic Tools[7] (globalEDGE 2016).

Companies contemplating their international expansion should evaluate the following priorities:

- Is the contemplated expansion a good strategic fit with the company's background, organizational culture, and existing strategic mission?

---

[7] globalEDGE (2016) offers a range of trade-related assessment tools on a fee basis. CORE is a self-assessment tool that allows to determine company's readiness to expand its operations internationally and ascertain its ability to export a particular product. PARTNER is an interactive tool that assists in evaluating and comparing a variety of potential international venture partners. DISTRIBUTOR is designed to aid companies in identifying the best distributor or agent to use specific to their product and market characteristics when opening up to new markets. FREIGHT evaluates the compatibility of international freight forwarders with the company business.

- Does it enhance the company's strategic strengths and mitigate its weaknesses?
- Are there sufficient internal and external resources available for expansion?
- What are the short-term and long-term business benefits, costs, and risks associated with expansion? How do they balance against each other in the overall context? Do the benefits outweigh the costs and risks in the case of action versus no action?
- Which countries, markets, or global regions should be targeted in the first order of priority?
- What is the best entry mode/strategy for international expansion?
- Should the company expand early or late?
- Should the expansion be pursued on a small or large scale?
- Some additional considerations may address further entrepreneurial start-up processes and dynamics, operational logistics, and growth in their entrepreneurial and managerial aspects, as well as strategies for steering the business through stages of growth, maturity, and eventually deciding on a possible market exit.

In the following, we discuss several analytical tools, frameworks, sources of information, and assistance instrumental in addressing some of these questions.

International Expansion and the Company Mission

Going international is a serious strategic endeavor with high stakes, resource commitments, sunk costs, and risks involved. Such a move, if undertaken, should be consistent with the company's background, organizational culture, current mission, and future vision in the growth context. Companies that are not fit to go international under their mission, lack international experience in their "DNA," or suffer weak top management commitment and support are likely to fail.

Enhancing Company's Strengths and Mitigating Weaknesses

A contemplated overseas expansion makes sense if it facilitates a company's strengths and mitigates weaknesses identified in the SWOT and other analyses. At least, the expansion should not significantly worsen the company's strategic competitive position.

Availability and Access to Corporate Resources

Overseas expansion is often an entrepreneurial or intrapreneurial[8] undertaking, a start-up. It requires substantial investment of valuable corporate time, financial and material resources, and talent and managerial expertise. It also presumes leveraging a company's core competencies difficult to replicate by overseas competitors, access to material and financial resources to tap into, qualified, internationally experienced, and committed personnel, and others. Three critical factors of success in international expansion are: availability of competitive product/service ensuring consumer demand, effective international marketing mix (popularly known as the 4Ps of marketing), and top corporate management commitment and support for overseas expansion.

Benefits, Costs, and Risks of International Expansion

Every step in business involves start-up, operational, tactical, and strategic benefits, costs, and risks. All other things equal, companies strive to maximize their business benefits, minimize costs, and mitigate risks. To act, or not to act? That is the question. As the adage goes, if it isn't broke, don't fix it. Although inaction might often seem attractive as a short-term strategic alternative, doing nothing may still be fraught with missed business opportunities, loss of competitiveness in the ever-changing business landscape, and has its own costs and risks. "Pretending your job is safe and your company is stable leaves you dangerously exposed. If you think risk taking is risky, being risk averse is often riskier" (Rottenberg 2014).

---

[8] Intrapreneurship is the act of behaving like an entrepreneur while working within a large organization.

Strategic Benefits

Strategic benefits that companies strive to achieve in their international expansion differ, depending on whether this expansion pursues overseas *marketing* or overseas *manufacturing*. In general, *marketing-related* overseas expansion gravitates toward countries with high gross domestic product (GDP) per capita, which signifies high spending power, and a large population, which signifies a large consumer/customer base, and other factors (e.g., positive market perception of the product, cultural proximity between the host and the home country) that make the host (foreign) country an attractive target market. In contrast, *manufacturing-related* overseas expansion is often driven by strategic efficiency through utilization of cheap local factors of production—labor, minerals, energy, land, and so on—in a host country.

More specifically, overseas expansion translates into the following potential *strategic benefits* stemming from a global or geo-regional scale: increase in market share, sales, and profits; advance corporate competitiveness and brand; gain access to cheap factors of production and resources (mineral resources, labor, capital, energy, etc.); diversify geographically and reduce dependence on existing markets; and achieve geographic proximity to important global markets when product shipping costs from the manufacturing site to the market are prohibitively high. It also allows companies to extend the sales potential of existing product lines by expanding the marketing life cycle overseas; exploit existing corporate technology, intellectual property, proprietary know-how, or managerial core competencies as competitive advantages; stabilize seasonal market fluctuations; mitigate temporary excessive production capacity hard to realize domestically; and gather intelligence about foreign competition by probing their defenses through overseas offenses. Other benefits include the ability to escape intensity of domestic competition; sharpen competitive edge by engaging in global competition; escape tight domestic business regulations or bad corporate image (an increasingly challenging task under the fast evolving global electronic media); take competitive advantage of the economy of scale, and others.

Along with a wide availability of commercial research databases specific to companies, industries, and countries, there are also electronic sources for free public access that can be used as a starting point in international business research. One of them is the globalEDGE portal, a mega depository containing research information, and analytical and decision-making tools for international business. The globalEDGE's annual Market Potential Index[9] (MPI) for 2016 provides global rankings for 87 countries worldwide categorized under eight criteria: market size, market intensity, market growth rate, market consumption capacity, commercial infrastructure, market receptivity, economic freedom, country risk, and overall score. Table 1.1 provides a fragment from MPI 2016 comparing Russia's market attractiveness with the BRICS (Brazil, Russia, India, China, and South Africa) countries. Depending on the specific goal of the overseas expansion, the company can rationalize its selection of the best target markets by conducting comparative analysis of the global rankings under the chosen specific parameter or several parameters.

In addition to the MPI country index, globalEDGE also publishes annual global indices for the following industries: advanced manufacturing, alternative energy, automotive electronics and composites/lightweight materials, biosciences, chemicals, food processing, land-based products, machinery, and medical devices. As its name suggests, the MPI index provides only a general picture, not thorough analytical information/analysis sufficient for decision making on overseas expansion; industries vary in their profitability, strategic drivers and constraints, trends, cost structure, and other dynamics. Therefore, decisions like this involve gathering business intelligence resultant from comprehensive specialized

---

[9] Global marketing has become more and more important over the years with the increasing trend of internationalization. Faced with too many choices, marketers have the challenge of determining which international markets to enter and the appropriate marketing strategies for those countries. The purpose of this study is to rank, with a U.S. focus, the market potential of 87 identified countries and to provide guidance to the U.S. companies that plan to expand their markets internationally. While the United States is not included in the rankings, the insights provided by the index are still applicable to companies located in other international markets. Eight dimensions are chosen to represent the market potential of a country on a scale of 1 to 100. The dimensions are measured using various indicators, and are weighted in determining their contribution to the overall Market Potential Index (MPI).

Table 1.1 *Market potential index 2016 (Russia versus BRICS countries)*

Country	Overall MPI rank, out of 87	Scores on specific MPI criteria, from 1 (lowest potential) to 100 (highest potential)							
		Market size	Market growth rate	Market intensity	Market consumption capacity	Commercial infrastructure	Economic freedom	Market receptivity	Country risk
China	1	100	95	1	92	62	22	7	78
India	4	37	78	32	66	28	45	7	76
Russia	35	18	51	42	58	49	24	7	39
Brazil	20	17	59	48	47	40	49	5	56
S. Africa	79	5	46	43	1	47	55	10	56

Source: globalEDGE (2016).

international market research and industry and country-specific consulting assistance.

Costs

Costs associated with overseas expansion vary. For example, industries, due to their economic dynamics, may be labor-intensive, capital-intensive, land-intensive, or energy-intensive. The cost of doing business across countries also differs due to the differences in their economic geography and climate, business environment, mineral resource endowment, infrastructure, and operational efficiency. Additionally, it depends on the company's entry strategy and mode of operation. For example, in case of *exporting*, the cargo shipping, tariffs, insurance, and some other items constitute major expenditures over and above the product manufacturing cost. An overseas *manufacturing* project under the "green field" investment or the international joint venture format may involve sizeable long-term financing requirements, home and host country personnel commitment, and a large-scale capital asset allocation. Entering an international licensing or franchising agreement is less capital-intensive, but may involve considerable legal fees and intellectual property protection expenditures. The costs of overseas expansion are also highly dependent on the company's management and operational efficiency.

KPMG, a U.S.-based global consultancy, publishes the biannual "Competitive Alternatives" report that contains comprehensive comparative cost information for international business locations. The report explores the most significant business cost factors in more than 100 cities and 10 countries around the world. This study measures and provides insight on the impact of 26 key cost components, across 7 business to business service segments, and 12 significant manufacturing sectors. A company contemplating its overseas manufacturing-driven expansion can rationalize its expansion decision by comparing and contrasting industry costs across countries and cities. For example, a comparative national cost index for the Professional Services sector/International Financial Services industry is computed in the KPMG report as follows: U.S. = 100 percent; UK = 86.7 percent (a 13.3 percentage point cost advantage over the United States); Japan = 85.6 percent; France = 82.8

percent; Germany = 81.4 percent; Italy = 80.3 percent; Australia = 78.3 percent; The Netherlands = 77.3 percent; Canada = 72.4 percent; and Mexico = 56.9 percent ("Competitive Alternatives" 2016). Thus from the cost minimization perspective Mexico and Canada present the most attractive options for the International Financial Services industry.

Another useful analytical tool for comparative global cost assessment is the annual "Doing Business" report by the World Bank. The latest (2016) "Doing Business" survey provides an assessment on the ease and cost of doing business across 189 countries worldwide and the following 10 parameters/business topics: starting a business, dealing with construction permits, getting electricity, registering property, getting credit, protecting minority investors, paying taxes, trading across borders, enforcing contracts, and resolving insolvency. Additionally, the user can obtain country information on labor market regulations.

Risks

Risks are an integral part of domestic and international business. International business risks tend to be more complex and potent compared to domestic risks due to geographic distances, cross-country variations in political-economic and legal systems, divergences in judicial systems, cultural discrepancies, language and communication barriers, chance events such as natural disasters, wars, political upheavals, financial-economic crises, sudden changes in government, and others. Owing to their nature and complexity, many risks in international business are hard to predict and harder yet to avoid.

While business risks cannot be eliminated completely, they can be mitigated through preliminary background research, intelligence gathering, due diligence, country selection characterized by low risks, choosing the right entry strategy, finding the right partners and fostering their trust and commitment, establishing transparent and efficient operating procedures, engaging in foreign currency exchange hedging, and building lasting personal relations.

Information on risk analysis and assessment can be obtained from numerous electronic databases such as Business Source Complete, LexisNexis, Business Insights Global, GMID/Euromonitor/Passport,

ABI/INFORM, to name a few. More specific risk assessment information and useful financial analysis related to risks can be obtained from such publications as the Almanac of Business and Industrial Financial Ratios, Handbook of Industry Profiles, and Standard & Poor's Industry Surveys. These and other databases can be accessed through university libraries or other channels.

A good starting step in international business risk assessment may be to analyze the country and industry risk profiles in publications and other reports by large insurance companies that serve global corporate clientele. These companies provide up-to-date country risk assessments based on sophisticated statistical models and comprehensive macroeconomic databases. The next chapter gives some examples of the risk assessment for Russia by three global insurance companies: the Belgian-based Credendo Group (a.k.a. Office National du Ducroire—ONDD) 2016), a credit insurance firm with direct presence in 13 countries and risk assessment coverage for 246 countries worldwide; the French-based Coface Group, a firm with direct presence in 66 countries and risk evaluation coverage for 158 countries (2016); and the U.S.-based AM Best Rating and Criteria Center (2016) that provides risk assessment profiles for 107 countries worldwide.

The annual Global Competitiveness Report (GCR) 2015–2016 (2015)[10] by the Swiss-based World Economic Forum is another useful analytical and decision-making tool that can be used for country/market selection designated for international expansion. On the one hand, analytical information presented in this report portrays global competitiveness by country. On the other hand, the better the country's global rankings are, the more efficient and attractive its position is likely to be from the international business standpoint. More specifically, the country's strong

---

[10] Global Competitiveness Report framework available complimentary online incorporates 12 "pillars of competitiveness": institutions, infrastructure, macroeconomic environment, health and primary education, higher education and training, goods market efficiency, labor market efficiency, financial market development, technological readiness, market size, business sophistication, and innovation. The latest report covers 140 countries.

rankings in global competitiveness tend to correlate with its attractiveness for exporting and foreign direct investments.

Another useful analytical-assessment tool in national global competitiveness is the annual World Competitiveness Yearbook (WCY) by the Swiss-based International Institute for Management Development IMD.[11] The basic version of WCY offers limited information with complimentary online access. More comprehensive country reports from WCY can be obtained for a fee.

---

[11] WCY analyzes and ranks the ability of nations to create and maintain an environment that sustains the competitiveness of enterprises. It means that WCY assumes that wealth creation takes place primarily at enterprise level (whether private or state-owned)—in WCY this field of research is called: "competitiveness of enterprises." However, enterprises operate in a national environment that enhances or hinders their ability to compete domestically or internationally—in WCY this field of research is called: "competitiveness of nations." Based on analysis made by leading scholars and by WCY's own research and experience, the methodology of the WCY divides the national environment into four main factors: economic performance, government efficiency, business efficiency, and infrastructure. In turn, each of these factors is divided into five subfactors that highlight every facet of the areas analyzed. Altogether, the WCY features 20 such subfactors. These 20 subfactors comprise more than 300 criteria, although each subfactor does not necessarily have the same number of criteria (for example, it takes more criteria to assess Education than to evaluate Prices). Each subfactor, independently of the number of criteria it contains, has the same weight in the overall consolidation of results that is 5% ($20 \times 5 = 100$). Criteria can be hard data, which analyze competitiveness as it can be measured (e.g., GDP) or soft data, which analyze competitiveness as it can be perceived (e.g., availability of competent managers). Hard criteria represent a weight of 2/3 in the overall ranking whereas the survey data represent a weight of 1/3. In addition, some criteria are for background information only, which means that they are not used in calculating the overall competitiveness ranking (e.g., population under 15). Finally, aggregating the results of the 20 subfactors makes the total consolidation, which leads to the overall ranking of the WCY. WCY claims its superiority over Global Competitiveness Report (GCR) by the World Economic Forum by covering 300 indicators compared to only 120 indicators in GCR and a much greater reliance on hard data compared to interviews/questionnaires in GCR.

Which Countries, Markets, or Global Regions Should Be Targeted As a Priority?

There are around two hundred nations around the world, each of them characterized by its unique geographic and political-economic conditions, laws and regulatory environment, physical and business infrastructure, climate, cultural customs and business practices. Under resource constraints, the company's international expansion should prioritize country selection in a pursuit of the right mix of strategic benefits, costs, and risks. Meanwhile, simultaneous expansion to multiple countries may be a bad decision: It stretches company resources thin and is often fraught with failure due to expansive costs and risks involved in multicountry expansion.

Due to dissimilarities in drivers and dynamics between marketing-related and manufacturing-related overseas expansion alternatives, the approaches for selecting target countries in these cases differ. A *marketing-driven expansion* is relatively less complex, less costly, and less risky than a manufacturing-driven expansion. A typical export transaction by and large involves just shipping and logistics of goods and services, a process characterized by shorter time frames, smaller financial commitments, and limited risks. In contrast, a *manufacturing-driven expansion* may involve a sizeable foreign direct investment financial commitment, higher costs, liabilities, and risks, as well as complex logistics and management issues associated with expansion and operations in a host country.

There is a wide range of available manuals, tutorials, sources of information, and assistance[12] on exporting. In a pursuit of time and

---

[12] In addition and beyond the print and electronic library resources, international companies and entrepreneurs should engage consulting assistance. For example, the U.S. Department of Commerce (domestically): www.buyusa.gov/home/us.html; the U.S. Commercial Service (internationally): www.buyusa.gov/home/worldwide_us.html; the American Chamber (AmCham) of Commerce offices overseas, bilateral chamber of commerce (e.g., the German American Chamber of Commerce www.gaccsouth.com/en/); foreign government consulates and other agencies in the United States (many countries have their trade promotion offices in major U.S. cities); and international trade/marketing consultants. Many industries have their professional associations providing consulting services, maintaining information depositories, organizing networking events, and providing other support on international business.

cost-efficiency, companies contemplating their export-related international expansion may apply a "one stop shop" approach and start their exploration by tapping the most comprehensive sources enabling a background research. A case in point is the Los Angeles-based International Trade Compliance Institute (2016) database that offers complimentary access to a wide range of resources on international trade. Among them is the Four Stage Export Development Framework (Figure 1.2). The Framework designed by Maurice Kogon integrates the key stages of this process (Build Export Capacity→ Develop Export Markets→Make Sales/Get Paid→Deliver the Goods) and outlines necessary steps for each stage in the export development process.

The Export.gov[13] government portal (2016) is a mega depository hosting information and sources of assistance for U.S. exporters. One popular source in this information database is "A Basic Guide to Exporting" (2016), the official U.S. government resource for small- and medium-sized businesses. This source is available for public access, courtesy of the U.S. Department of Commerce.

A Basic Guide to Exporting contains a useful analytical tool, the Step-by-Step Approach to Market Research. The four prong step-by-step procedure from Basic Guide to Exporting summarized in the following lists key analytical and decision-making steps as well as sources of

---

[13] Export.gov is a major trade portal designated for helping American companies to succeed globally. Export.gov brings together resources from across the U.S. Government to assist American businesses in planning their international sales strategies. From market research and trade leads from the U.S. Department of Commerce's Commercial Service to export finance information from Export-Import Bank and the Small Business Administration to agricultural export assistance from USDA, Export.gov helps American exporters navigate the international sales process and avoid pitfalls such as nonpayment and intellectual property misappropriation. Export.gov was created to provide better customer service for businesses interacting with the Federal Government. The U.S. Department of Commerce's International Trade Administration manages Export.gov as a collaborative effort with the 19 Federal Agencies that offer export assistance programs and services.

Build Export Capacity	Develop Export Markets	Make Sales & Get Paid	Deliver the Goods
Improve Competitiveness	**Identify Best Markets**	**Close the Deal**	**Regulatory Compliance**
Situation analysis/SWOT Solidify fundamentals • Production processes • Business practices • Operating capital	Market research/analysis • Select target markets • Assess target markets · Competition · Market segments · Market conditions/partners	Respond to inquiries Quote prices-INCOTERMS Negotiate sales terms	U.S regulatory compliance Foreign regulatory compliance
Develop Export Readiness	**Develop Entry Strategies**	**Finance Sales Get Paid**	**Documentary Compliance**
Export readiness assessment Enhance company readiness • Export counseling • Export training &education	Market strategy planning • Distribution, pricing, and promotion • Adaptation/localization • Implementation/action plan • Resource/budget plan	Payment methods/services • Pre-export financing • Transaction financing • Export credit insurance • Factors and Forfeiters Payment Sources • Commercial Banks • Export-Import Bank • Factors and Forfeiters	U.S. documentary compliance Foreign documentary compliance
Get & Use Help	**Implement Strategy**		**Transport the Goods**
Trade assistance network • State export assistance centers • USDOC/USEACs & Embassies • County/city export centers • Chambers/Assoc./WTCs Trade assistance resources • Partner programs/services • Partner client databases • Internet trade sites	Find Partners • Trade leads • Int'l partner searches • Screen/select partners Promote export sales • Broadcast promotion • Targeted promotion • Market promotion financing		Manage the supply chain Prepare goods for delivery Book cargo/ship the goods

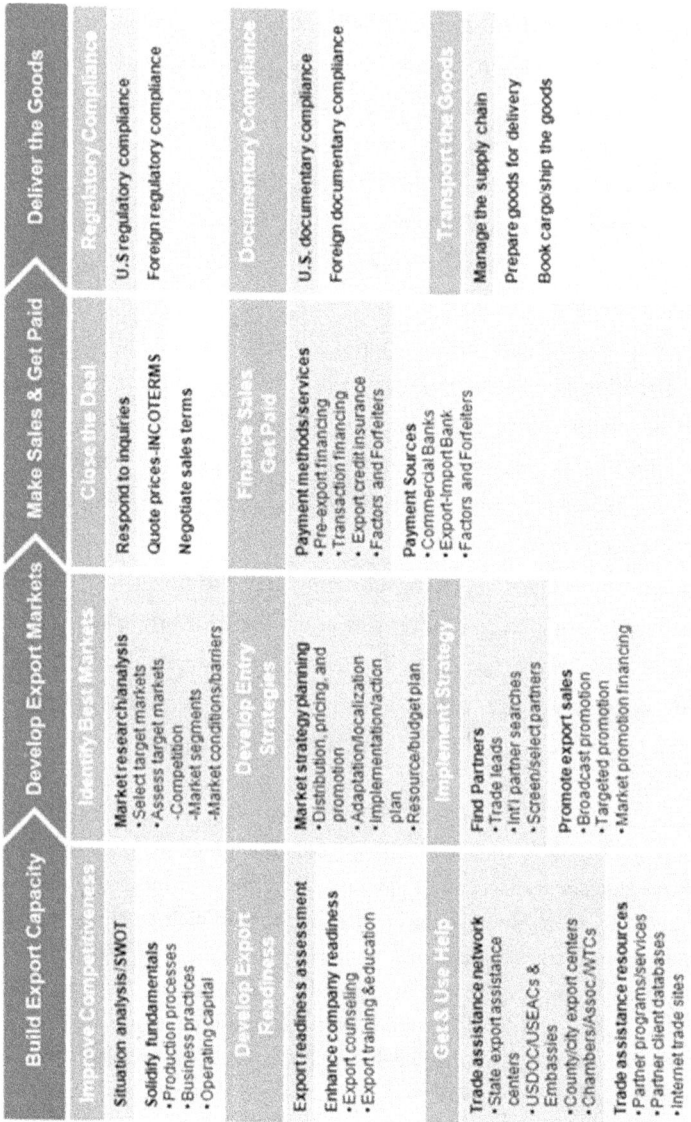

Figure 1.2 The four-stage export development framework

assistance enabling an exporting company to identify and strategically explore overseas target markets in the right order of priority.

Step-By-Step Approach to Market Research

Step 1. Find potential markets:

- Obtain trade statistics that indicate which countries import your type(s) of products.
- Perform a thorough review of the available market research reports in the country (ies) and industries in question to determine market openness, common practices, tariffs and taxes, distribution channels, and other important considerations.
- Identify 5 to 10 large and fast-growing markets for the firm's product(s). Analyze them over the past three to five years for market growth in good and bad times.
- Identify some smaller but fast-emerging markets where there may be fewer competitors.
- Target three to five of the most statistically promising markets for further assessment.
- Consult with a U.S. Export Assistance Center near you.

Step 2. Assess targeted markets:

- Examine consumption and production of competitive products, as well as overall demographic and economic trends in the target country.
- Ascertain the sources of competition, including the extent of domestic industry production and the major foreign countries the firm would compete against.
- Analyze factors affecting marketing and use of the product in each market, such as end-user sectors, channels of distribution, cultural idiosyncrasies, and business practices.

- Identify any foreign barriers (tariff or nontariff) for the product being imported into the country and identify any U.S. export controls.
- Identify U.S. or foreign incentives to promote exporting of your product or service.
- Determine whether your product is price-competitive after you've figured in packaging, shipping, marketing, sales commissions, taxes and tariffs, and other associated costs. See "pricing considerations."

Step 3. Draw conclusions

If the company is new to exporting, it is probably a good idea to target two or three markets initially. Your local Export Assistance Center can provide valuable insight into your "optimal" market opportunities.

Step 4. Test demand

There are a number of low-cost on-line and off-line services that can help new exporters gauge foreign market interest and collect overseas inquiries:

- Catalog exhibitions
- Commercial news USA/Export USA
- Foreign partner matching and trade lead services

As necessary, the step-by-step market research framework can be supplemented by analytical and decision-making tools designated for exporters from the Los Angeles Regional Export Council (2016).

Selecting a target country for manufacturing-related overseas expansion, whether it is a green field foreign investment or international acquisition, can be achieved through an exploration of business opportunities involving foreign investment and a comparative analysis of the investment climate across countries. Both these tasks can be accomplished and rationalized by applying the benefits-costs-risks framework. Owing to the high complexity and vast variety of information resources, we limit our discussion by just few sources.

- Country Commercial Guides (Export.gov 2016) and country portals by the U.S. Commercial Service (2016) are a must read for a company contemplating overseas expansion. Annual country commercial guides (Chapter 4) identify leading sectors for U.S. exports and investment—a good starting point. Country Commercial Guides (can be accessed via Export.gov portal) also offer a wide range of useful information and assistance on doing business in specific countries worldwide.

- The globalEDGE country portal (2016). Country information resources in this depository are organized around the following sections: Introduction, Statistics, Economy, History, Government, Culture, Risk, Corporations, Trade Statistics, Indices, Resources, Memo. Depending on the time, scope, and depth of analysis, the approach can vary from tapping short sections such as Memo or Introduction to a wider format including specialized sections and supplementary resources. The Indices section enables the user to generate a country's global rankings across more than a dozen parameters, thus providing a comparative profile and pointing out its attractiveness for business.

- "Investment Climate Statements" (2016). The latest available reports from this source cover 178 countries worldwide and are dense with useful factual information on the country business climate.

- The earlier-mentioned "Competitive Alternatives" (2016) biannual report by KPMG provides comparative cost-efficiency information across numerous countries, cities, and industries worldwide.

What Is the Best Entry Mode/Strategy Overseas?

After the company has identified a target country for expansion it should select an entry mode/strategy that ensures the best balance of strategic benefits, costs, and risks. Besides economic considerations such as profitability, return on investment, cost-efficiency, or market share, the choice of entry mode should ensure effective management and intellectual property protection. The latter is particularly critical for companies operating internationally whose competitive advantages lie in technologically sensitive products, services, or processes. The most common international

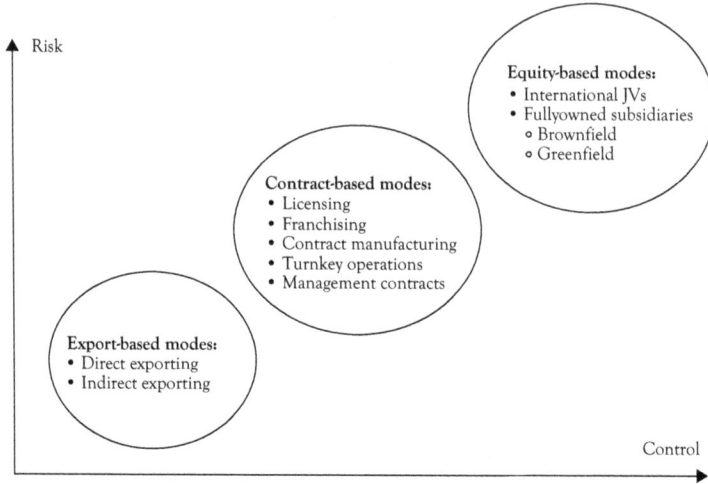

Figure 1.3 International entry modes

entry modes include: direct and indirect exporting/importing,[14] international licensing and franchising, international turnkey projects, wholly owned subsidiaries in the form of international greenfield investment and acquisition, joint ventures, and various strategic alliances. Each of these alternative entry modes is characterized by its own pros, cons, situational applicability, and constraints. Figures 1.3 and 1.4 profile some of these entry modes and their characteristics.

Should the Company Expand Early or Late?

There are some first-mover advantages associated with entering a market early. The first mover often creates an ability to preempt late entrants and capture consumer demand by establishing a brand name, developing customer loyalty, and scaling up operations. Another advantage is the ability to build up sales volume in that country and ride down the experience curve ahead of rivals. Additionally, it may give the first mover a cost advantage over the late entrants generated by economies of scale. This cost advantage may enable the early entrant to respond to the late entrant's

---

[14] For more specifics please refer to *A Basic Guide to Exporting* (2016).

MODE OF ENTRY	ADVANTAGES	DISADVANTAGES
Exporting	Low risk Easy market entry or exit Gain local market knowledge Bypass FDI restrictions	Tariffs and quotas Transportation costs Possible distributor relationship issues
Licensing	Low risk Fast market access Bypass regulations and tariffs Gain local market knowledge	Less control over market and revenues Intellectual property concerns Potential problems with licensees/future competitors
Franchising	Low financial risk Bypass regulations and tariffs Keep more control Gain local market knowledge	Less control over market and revenues Some loss of control over operations Potential franchisee relationship issues
Contract manufacturing	Low financial risk Save on manufacturing costs Flexibility of short term commitment Emphasis on marketing/sales	Less control over operations Less knowledge about local market Potential damage to brand/finances if human rights issues arise
Management contracts	Insider access to market Emphasis on firm's expertise Low financial risk	Limited profits and market access Potential copyright and intellectual property issues
Turnkey operations	Access to FDI-unfriendly markets No long term operational risks Emphasis on firm's expertise	Some financial risks Potential issues with partners/ infrastructure/ labor / profit repatriation
Joint ventures	Insider access to market High profit potential More control over operations Shared risks Gain knowledge from partner(s)	High investment of resources Potential issues between partners over control/contributions/goals, etc. More management levels Potential intellectual property issues
Fully owned subsidiaries	Full market access/acceptance Full control over operations/profits Bypass tariffs Diversify operations	High financial/resources investment High political and environmental risks Potential profits repatriation issues More management levels

Figure 1.4 Advantages and disadvantages of international modes of entry

arrival by cutting prices below their higher cost structure, thereby driving the late entrants out of the market. Yet another strategic advantage is the ability of early entrants to create high switching costs that tie consumers and customers to their products or services. High switching costs will make it difficult for later entrants to win business and compete.

On the other hand, early entrants face first-mover disadvantages that are sometimes referred to as the "pioneering costs." Pioneering costs are costs that an early entrant has to bear that a later entrant can avoid. Pioneering costs arise when a business environment in a foreign country is so different from that in a firm's home market that the enterprise has to devote considerable time, effort, and expense to learning the rules of the game. Pioneering costs include the costs of business failure if the firm, due to its ignorance of the foreign environment, makes some major mistakes. Pioneering costs also include the costs of promoting and establishing a product offering, including the cost of (re)educating local customers (Hill and Hult 2016).

Should the Expansion Be Completed on a Small or Large Scale?

In choosing between small- and large-scale alternatives in an overseas expansion, an intuitive solution tends to be leaning toward small scale; as a matter of common sense, this approach involves lower costs and risks of international exposure. Small-scale entry creates an advantage in allowing a company to learn about a foreign market while simultaneously limiting the firm's risk exposure to that market. In contrast, entering the market on a large scale often involves significant commitment of corporate capital, human talent, and other resources. It also entails large-scale risks. However, small-scale entry is fraught with at least two potential problems. First, in order to get an overseas business start-up off the ground the entrant needs to gain and sustain competitive momentum that may be hard to achieve on a small scale. Second, a small scale start-up can be easily tackled and crashed by deeply entrenched foreign and domestic competitors operating in the host country on a larger scale.

All things considered, early entrance is normally associated with a large scale of expansion; late entrance, depending on circumstances, can be pursued either on a small or large scale.

Countries on the Selection Radar

Driven by their pursuit of development and growth in the competitive marketplace, corporations look for opportunities and scan the global business environment. Varying in their strategic approaches, priorities, and managerial philosophies, corporations are not created equal. And yet, fundamentally, corporations tend to view the world, its global regions and countries in a utilitarian perspective through their strategic lenses as an ever-changing mix of strategic benefits/opportunities, costs/threats, and risks. Although country selection decisions in each particular case are motivated by unique strategic and operational conditions specific to the company, industry, business venture, or other situational circumstances, a general environmental assessment across countries has its own importance and analytical value in a comparative context. Country analysis can become a component of an international business/marketing plan specific to an expansion or investment project. As such, country analysis is an integral part of the three-prong international strategic evaluation framework: company analysis, industry analysis, and country analysis.

Marketing-Related Expansion

Earlier, we distinguished between two major types of overseas expansion: marketing-related expansion and manufacturing-related expansion. Marketing-related expansion (a foreign entry in this case can occur in the form of exporting, licensing, or franchising) tends to gravitate toward countries with large population, indicating large potential customer base, and high GDP/capita, indicating high spending power. Assuming that business decisions, fundamentally speaking, are rational and happen for a reason,[15] we can argue: attracted by profit maximization but constrained by limited availability of resources, companies operating in their respective product/service line niches will seek to prioritize their overseas expansion decisions and place their top preferences on the largest and fastest growing markets. Even without knowing specific market conditions and dynamics characterizing these largest and fastest growing markets, a decision maker can further rationalize: These markets—we will categorize them as target markets—for a given product/service line have proved to be robust attracting inflows of products/services from around the world over years to reach their current top ranks in the global order. An ideal target market should be both large in size and fast growing.

Large market size makes the target country attractive internationally because it holds high current potential for the new entrant's market expansion, increase in sales and revenues, improved global competitiveness through economies of scale and facilitates other strategic benefits as argued earlier. Meanwhile, some smaller but fast growing markets can

---

[15] Rationality in actual decision making is limited by the information managers or entrepreneurs have available, their cognitive limitations, and the finite time they have to make a decision. Additionally, as human beings, managers or entrepreneurs in their decisions are impacted by their demographics (e.g., age, gender), race, and ethnic affiliation, individual psychological traits (e.g., type A vs. type B, introvert vs. extravert), microgroup dynamics and macro organizational culture, personal emotions, likes and dislikes, and so on. All together that infuses in decision making a dose of irrationality.

also be strategically important; although today's relatively small market size by itself may be insufficient to justify a commitment of corporate resources for expansion to and development of this market, due to its fast growth rate and a stable robust growth pattern this market can become large and potent in the future perspective. Thus entering such a smaller but fast growing market today can be justified as a strategic development step toward the future.

Sometimes strategic analysts, corporate decision makers, and entrepreneurs find themselves grappling with the dilemma; some international markets are currently large, but stagnant or even have even been declining over recent years; on the other hand, other markets appear small at the moment but have been fast growing over recent years. Such a trade-off has no universal solution and requires an in-depth benefit/cost/risk analysis, as well as strategic vision and business acumen on the part of a decision maker.

Manufacturing-Related Expansion

A foreign entry in this case can occur in the form of contract manufacturing, management contract, turnkey operations, international joint venture, or fully owned subsidiary. This type of expansion strives for global strategic cost-efficiency and synergies. From this standpoint, potential foreign entrants to a target market/country look for availability and cost-efficiency of the local factors of production (e.g., land/all natural resources, labor/all human resources, capital/all man-made resources, and enterprise that integrates all these resources together under the manufacturing process. In a broader sense, foreign entrants are interested in many factors, including an efficient business infrastructure (e.g., transportation, communication, sewage, water, and electric systems), social infrastructure (health, education, housing, civic and utilities, transport, corrections and justice), and general and industry-specific regulatory environment (e.g., the laws, rules, and regulations put into place by federal, state, or other government entities and nongovernmental organizations (NGOs) to control the behavior and actions of business activities relevant to the industry). An efficient, business-friendly and stable political-economic environment, sound financial-banking system, and cultural similarities/proximity between the home and the host country, are also important factors to consider.

Proliferation of the Internet, electronic media, public sources, and commercial databases broadens country analysis opportunities and efficiency in the earlier context. Here are some examples of databases containing comprehensive up-to-date country information and analysis.

- The Trading Economics (2016) portal hosts statistical information on 196 countries, including historical data for more than 300,000 economic indicators, exchange rates, stock market indexes, government bond yields, and commodity prices. The complimentary data access is based on official sources, not third-party data providers.
- The World Factbook (2016), an annual publication by the U.S. Central Intelligence Agency (CIA), provides complimentary access to information on the history, people, government, economy, geography, communications, transportation, military, and transnational issues for 267 world entities.
- The globalEDGE (2016) is one of the world's largest depositories of international business information in complimentary access. Its Global Insights section contains international business and trade information on over 200 countries, the 50 U.S. states, as well as nearly two dozen industry sectors, and numerous regional trade blocs.
- Business Monitor International (BMI), commercially subscribed database, offers independent analysis and forecasts on countries, industries, and financial markets. BMI integrates country risk and industry analysis and forecasts on global, regional, and country-level developments and trends across 200 countries and 24 industry verticals.
- CountryWatch, a commercially subscribed database, provides country-specific intelligence and data. Key publications produced by CountryWatch include the CountryReviews, an up-to-date series of publications for each country including demographic, political, economic, business, cultural and environmental information, and the CountryWire, which

provides daily news coverage for every country in the world and a significant news archive made up of the compendium of regional news carriers.

- Economist Intelligence Unit (EIU), a commercially sub-scribed database, covers a wide range of countries, industries, and issues. EIU's flagship Country Report publication provides political and economic analysis and forecasts for 197 countries. It examines and explains the important political and economic trends and developments in each country. Country Reports include the EIU's core outlook for each country, which provides a five-year forecast of political and policy trends and major economic variables. Possible risks to political stability are highlighted as well. Corporations use the Country Report to analyze international entry strategies, develop an international business strategy, identify opportunities and risks, keep abreast of international developments for current operations or negotiations, and compare reports from local staff.

- IHS Global, a commercially subscribed database, provides a holistic view of the economic and risk environment in over 200 countries with daily analysis, detailed country profiles, transparent risk ratings, and economic forecasts that cover up to 500 indicators per economy.

- Passport (a.k.a. Euromonitor International and GMID), a commercially subscribed database, is one of the best global market research databases. It provides statistics, analysis, reports, surveys, and breaking news on industries, countries, and consumers worldwide. Passport connects market research to the company goals and annual planning, analyzing market context, competitor insight, and future trends impacting businesses globally. Passport offers detailed analysis of consumer and industrial markets around the world across 781 cities, 210 countries, and 27 industries with historic data from 1997 and forecasts through 2020. Passport data is cross-country comparable.

- Major global institutions such as the International Monetary Fund (IMF), World Bank, World Trade Organization (WTO), United Nations Conference on Trade and Development (UNCTAD), Organization for Economic Cooperation and Development (OECD) also offer, in their respective domains, annual global, country/region-specific, and topical reports for free public access.
- National government and private sources and databases also provide useful business country specific information and analysis. For example, Russia-based РосБизнесКонсалтинг[16] (РБК), an information agency, provides commercially subscribed database "РБК.Исследования рынков" (РБК. Market Research). The РБК depository claims to include some 9,000 market research reports, business plans, databases, analyses, and more. It should be noted however, that using local sources may involve language barriers and credibility issues.

Owing to the tremendous volume and high complexity of information presented in international business reports, corporate analysts and decision makers as well as entrepreneurs may find it beneficial to use country reports that contain both factual information and analysis rather than mining raw statistical and factual information from primary sources (national statistical agencies and global institutions), to conduct their own customized analysis in-house.

References

AM Best Rating and Criteria Center. 2016. www3.ambest.com/ratings/

A Basic Guide to Exporting. 2016. www.export.gov/article?id=Why-Companies-should-export

Coface Group. 2016. www.coface-usa.com/Economic-studies

"Competitive Alternatives." 2016. KPMG. www.competitivealternatives.com/reports/compalt2016_report_vol1_en.pdf

Credendo Group. 2016. www.delcredereducroire.be/en/country-risks/

---

[16] RosBiznesConsulting (Russian Business Consulting).

"Doing Business." 2016. World Bank. www.doingbusiness.org/reports

Elkington, J. 1997. *Cannibals with Forks: The Triple Bottom Line of Twenty-First Century Business.* Oxford: Capstone. http://appli6.hec.fr/amo/Public/Files/Docs/148_en.pdf

Export.gov. 2016. "Step-by-Step Guide to Market Research." www.export.gov/article?id=Step-by-Step-Guide

Export.gov. 2016b. "Country Commercial Guides." www.export.gov/ccg

Friedman, M. 1970. "The Social Responsibility of Business is to Increase its Profits." *Times Magazine,* September 13: 32–33, pp. 122–24.

GlobalEDGE. 2016. http://globaledge.msu.edu/

Global Competitiveness Report 2015–2016. 2015. "World Economic Forum." www3.weforum.org/docs/gcr/2015-2016/Global_Competitiveness_Report_2015-2016.pdf

Hill, C., and T. Hult. 2016. *Global Business Today.* 9th ed. New York: McGraw-Hill.

Hill, C.W., G.R. Jones, and M.A. Schilling. 2015. *Strategic Management: Theory: an Integrated Approach.* 8th ed. Boston: Cengage Learning.

International Trade Compliance Institute. 2016. "Trade Information Database." www.tradecomplianceinstitute.org/p_trade_info_db_links.php?SubCatID=2&Cat=Trade%20Readiness%20Tools&SubCat=Export%20Guides

"Investment Climate Statements." 2016. U.S. Department of State. www.state.gov/e/eb/rls/othr/ics/

Los Angeles Regional Export Council. 2016. "Begin Exporting." http://larexc.org/export/begin-exporting/

Porter, M., and M. Kramer. 2011. "Creating Shared Value." *Harvard Business Review.* January–February 2011. https://hbr.org/2011/01/the-big-idea-creating-shared-value

Rottenberg, L. 2014. *Crazy Is a Compliment: The Power of Zigging When Everyone Else Zags.* London: Portfolio Hardcover.

Trading Economics. 2016. www.tradingeconomics.com

U.S. Commercial Service. 2016. "International U.S. Commercial Service Offices." http://2016.export.gov/worldwide_us/index.asp

World Factbook. 2016. "Central Intelligence Agency." www.cia.gov/library/publications/the-world-factbook/

CHAPTER 2

Russia

Attractiveness in a Global Perspective

Do not expect that once taking advantage of Russia's weakness, you will receive dividends forever. Russians have always come for their money. And when they come—do not rely on an agreement signed by you, you are supposed to justify. Therefore, with the Russians it is to play fair, or do not play.

—Otto von Bismarck
(1815–1898; First Chancellor of Germany)

Main Points in This Chapter

- Russia's macroeconomic profile, drivers, and dynamics.
- Strategic strengths and weaknesses in the comparative global context.
- Market attractiveness, ease, and risks of doing business.
- Leading sectors for U.S. exports and investment.

Russia's Macroeconomic Profile, Drivers, and Dynamics

Russia is the world's largest geographic area and a major economy. As of 2015, Russia had a population of 142.4 million people, comprising 1.8 percent of the world's population and placing it 10th out of 238 countries worldwide. It registered $3.718 trillion in gross domestic product (GDP), purchasing power parity, comprising 2.8 percent of the world total and placing the nation 7th out of 230. Russian GDP per capita, an integrative measure of economic performance, reached $25,400 in purchasing power parity, 73rd out of 230. Exports were at $337.8 billion, 1.8 percent of the world total, giving the nation a global rank of 15th out of 224. In contrast, Russia's life expectancy at birth for the total population, a key measure of social development, was only 70.47 years (sandwiched between Kazakhstan and Moldova), a dismal 153rd out of the 224 countries in the world (Central Intelligence Agency 2016). Russia's rank in the Yale University's Environmental Performance Index (Hsu 2016) was 32nd out of 180. Its rank in the Human Development Index (Human Development Report 2015) was 50th out of 188, steadily rising at an annual average of 0.38 percent between 1990 and 2014. Adding to this picture is Russia's 56th out of 157 rank in the World Happiness Report (Helliwell et al. 2016). Over the past few centuries, Russia has been evolving as a major regional economic, military, and political force, while remaining relatively isolated in the global perspective geographically, politically, and economically (Zhuplev 2008).[1] After the dissolution of the U.S.S.R. in the early 1990s and a turbulent post-Soviet transition, Russia, as the largest successor state, is striving to regain its lost power status and restore its premier role as a geo-regional actor.

Historically, energy and commodities—particularly oil, natural gas, metals, and timber—have played paramount roles in Russia's domestic economy and foreign policy. Russia's economy is highly dependent on exports of commodities with crude oil, petroleum products, and natural gas accounting for 68 percent of total shipments. In 2015, trade surplus dropped significantly due to a steep plunge in oil prices and economic sanctions imposed by Europe and United States following the Ukraine crisis. In 2015, about half of the country's federal budget revenue came from sales of crude oil, petroleum products, and natural gas. Other main exports include fuels and energy products (63 percent of total shipments, of which crude oil and natural gas accounted for 26 percent and 12 percent, respectively), metals, machinery and equipment, chemical products, and foodstuffs and agricultural products. Russia's main export partners in 2015 were: the Netherlands (11.9 percent), China (8.3 percent), Germany

---

[1] Russia's global political-economic isolation has been deepening since 2014 because of Russian annexation of the Crimea followed by military hostilities in Southern Ukraine, Western sanctions, political confrontations in Syria, plane-downing incident by Turkey and Russia's own countersanctions, self-autarky policies, and politics.

(7.4 percent), Italy (6.5 percent), Turkey (5.6 percent), Belarus (4.4 percent), and Japan (4.2 percent) (Central Intelligence Agency 2016).

Since the dissolution of the Soviet Union, Russia has undergone significant changes. While moving from a globally isolated, centrally planned economy toward a more market-based and globally integrated economy, it has stalled due to a partially reformed, statist economy with a high concentration of wealth in officials' hands. Economic reforms in the 1990s privatized most industry, with notable exceptions in the energy and defense-related sectors. The private sector remains subject to heavy state interference. Russia is one of the world's leading producers of oil and natural gas and is a top exporter of metals such as steel and primary aluminum. Its manufacturing sector, however, is generally uncompetitive on world markets and leans toward domestic consumption. Russia's reliance on commodity exports makes it vulnerable to boom and bust cycles that follow the volatile swings in global prices. The economy, which averaged 7 percent growth between 1998 and 2008 as oil prices rose rapidly, was one of the hardest hit by the 2008–2009 global economic crisis, as oil prices plummeted and foreign credits that Russian banks and firms relied on dried up. Declining oil prices over the past few years and difficulty attracting foreign direct investment have contributed to a noticeable slowdown in GDP growth rates. In late 2013, the Russian Economic Development Ministry reduced its growth forecast through 2030 to an average of only 2.5 percent per year, down from its previous forecast of 4.0 to 4.2 percent. In 2014, following Russia's military intervention in Ukraine and subsequent international sanctions, grouped with declining oil prices, pushed Russia into a recession with overall GDP growth into negative territory to –3.7 percent in 2015. The Russian Ministry of Economic Development forecasts modest positive GDP growth of 0.7 percent in 2016 (Central Intelligence Agency 2016). However, the World Bank is predicting a further contraction of –1.9 percent in 2016, followed by modest growth of 1.1 percent in 2017. Figure 2.1 and Tables 2.1 and 2.2 provide some of Russia's key macroeconomic indicators.[2]

---

[2] More details and macroeconomic analysis can be obtained from: Trading Economics/Russia (2016); Economic Intelligence Unit. September (2016).

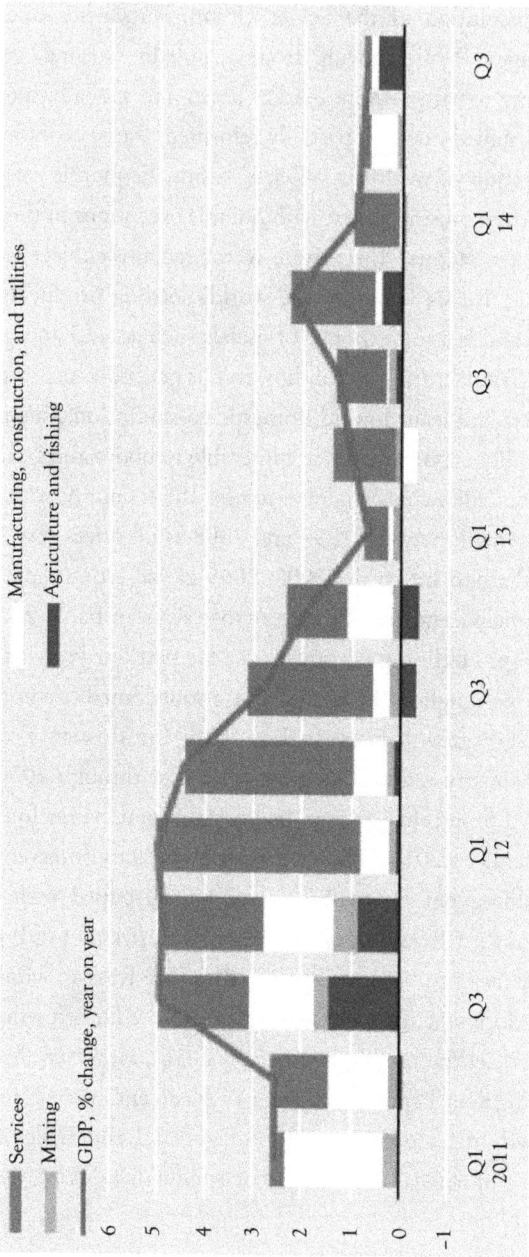

Figure 2.1 Russia: GDP growth by economic sectors, percentage point contribution

Source: Economic Intelligence Unit (2015, 29).

Table 2.1 *Russia: Annual data and forecast*

Indicators	2013[a]	2014[a]	2015[a]	2016[b]	2017[b]
GDP					
Nominal GDP, US$ bn	2,226.6	2.027.0	1,324.5	1,211.0	1,481.5
Real GDP growth, percent	1.2	0.7	–3.7	–0.8	0.7
Expenditure of GDP, percent real change					
Private consumption	4.3	1.5	–9.4	–2.6	1.2
Government consumption	1.4	0.2	–1.8	–1.5	–1.0
Gross fixed investment	1.3	–2.0	–7.7	–5.0	0.5
Exports of goods and services	4.6	0.7	3.5	–2.2	–0.2
Imports of goods and services	3.7	–7.4	–25.7	–11.6	2.2
Origin of GDP, percent real change					
Agriculture	4.7	2.0	2.9	1.1	1.8
Industry	0.6	0.1	–3.6	0.7	1.2
Services	1.6	1.2	–3.9	–1.7	0.4
Population and income					
Population, m	143.4	146.3	146.5	146.5	146.4
GDP per head, US$ at PPP	24,143	25,009	24,410	24,681	25,318
Fiscal indicators, percent of GDP					
Central government revenue	18.4	18.6	16.9	15.4	15.7
Central government expenditure	18.8	19.1	19.4	19.0	18.0
Central government balance	–0.5	0.4	–2.4	–3.7	–2.2
Total public debt	9.0	9.5	9.4	13.2	14.6
Prices and financial indicators					
Exchange rate Rb: US$, end-period	32.73	56.26	72.88	61.43	60.22

(Continued)

Table 2.1 Russia: Annual data and forecast   (Continued)

Indicators	2013[a]	2014[a]	2015[a]	2016[b]	2017[b]
Exchange rate Rb: €, end-period	44.97	68.34	79.70	67.27	65.80
Consumer prices, end-period, percent	6.8	7.8	15.5	7.2	5.7
Stock of broad money, percent change	6.6	7.9	-2.5	11.2	9.8
Lending interest rate, average, percent	9.5	11.1	15.7	12.7	10.0
Current account, US$ m					
Goods: exports fob	523,835	496,807	341,467	260,419	301,705
Goods: imports fob	−341,269	−307,875	−192,955	−167,190	−172,653
Services balance	−58,259	−55,278	−36,875	−26,377	−23,599
External debt, US$ m					
Debt stock	727,544[c]	600,960[c]	520,185[c]	517,746	506,626
Debt service paid	73,886[c]	137,453[c]	92,380[c]	76,003	85,232
Principal repayments	56,857[c]	118,203[c]	76,225[c]	61,524	70,704
Total international reserves, US$ m	509,593	385,459	368,398	367,916	383,983

Source: Economic Intelligence Unit (2016e, 11).

Note: [a] Actual. [b] Economist Intelligence Unit forecasts. [c] Fiscal years (beginning April 1st of year indicated).

Figure 2.1 reveals a somewhat volatile pattern of Russia's macroeconomic growth: a 2.5 percent annual GDP growth rate in early 2011 jumps to 5 percent in late 2011 to early 2012. It then drops to less than 1 percent in early 2013, rises to 2 percent in late 2013, only to start declining again afterward. Another aspect of this volatility as presented in Figure 2.1 is an uneven pattern in GDP growth contribution across the key sectors of the Russian economy—services, mining, manufacturing, and utilities. For example, services account for a sizeable share of contribution in GDP growth as of late 2011. Services' share remains dominant from 2012 to 2013, but drastically declines to become miniscule in 2014.

Table 2.2 Russia versus BRIC and "Aspirational" comparators, actual, 2015

Indicators	BRIC "Peer" countries				"Aspirational" comparator countries	
	Russia	Brazil	China	India	U.S.	Germany
GDP						
Nominal GDP, US$ bn	1,324.5	1,772.3	11,181	2,072	18,037	3,362
Real GDP growth, percent	−3.7	−3.8	6.9	7.5	2.6	1.3
Expenditure of GDP, percent real change						
Private consumption	−9.4	−4.0	8.4c	7.4	2.2	1.4
Government consumption	−1.8	1.0	9.7a	2.2	1.8	2.0
Gross fixed investment	−7.7	−14.1	5.9a	4.0	4.0	1.4
Exports of goods and services	3.5	6.1	0.8a	−5.2	0.1	3.5
Imports of goods and services	−25.7	−14.3	1.3a	−2.8	4.6	4.6
Population and income						
Population, m	146.5	204.5	1,361a	1,311	321.3	82.5
GDP per head, US$ at PPP	24,410	15,610a	14,677a	6,086b	56.129	49,950

(Continued)

Table 2.2 *Russia versus BRIC and "Aspirational" comparators, actual, 2015*   (Continued)

Indicators	BRIC "Peer" countries				"Aspirational" comparator countries	
	Russia	Brazil	China	India	U.S.	Germany
Prices and financial indicators						
Consumer prices, average, percent	15.5	10.7	1.7	4.9	0.1	1.6
Lending interest rate, average, percent	15.7	44.0	4.4	10.0	3.3	1.8
Current account, US$ m						
Goods: exports fob	341,467	190,092	2,142.8	272,353	1,510	1,368
Goods: imports fob	–192,955	–172,422	–1,575.8	–409,238	–2,273	–1,075
Services balance	–36,875	–36,919	–182.4	73,635	262	–39
External debt, US$ m						
Debt stock	520,185	542,296[a]	958.3[a]	488,447[b]	NA	NA
Debt service paid	92,380	91,562[a]	81.3[a]	47,329[b]	NA	NA
Principal repayments	76,225	NA	49.8[a]	35,831[b]	NA	NA
Total international reserves, US$ m	368,398	356,464	3,406.1	351,551	118,000	NA

Sources: Economic Intelligence Unit (2016e, 11); Economic Intelligence Unit (2016a, 11); Economic Intelligence Unit (2016b, 10); Economic Intelligence Unit (2016c, 11); Economic Intelligence Unit (2016d, 11).

Note: [a]Fiscal years (beginning April 1st of year indicated). [b]Economist Intelligence Unit estimates.

During 2014, the share of manufacturing's contribution shrank, while shares of agriculture and fishing rose significantly in Q3.

In 2015, Russia's GDP as a measure of absolute economic power stood lower than that of Brazil, China, and India, its peers in the BRIC group. This indicator was well below that of the United States and Germany, Russia's "aspirational" comparators. Russia's speed of economic development expressed in the GDP growth rate (−3.7 percent in 2015) was trailing behind its fellow BRIC countries, with the exception of Brazil. It was also lower compared to the United States and Germany. Additionally, Russia suffered higher inflation and had a higher lending interest rate compared to its BRIC peers, with the exception of Brazil. On a positive side, Russia's GDP per head as a measure of the nation's relative economic power fared significantly better than that of Brazil, China, and India, although trailing by a wide margin behind the United States and Germany (Table 2.2).

After the dissolution of the U.S.S.R. and gaining a sovereign status in the early 1990s, Russia experienced two severe economic crises in 1998 and 2008. In its recovery from the 2008 crisis, the Russian economy over the past five years (in 2015–2016 Russia continues to experience negative and stagnant macroeconomic dynamics) has been growing faster than the world average and that of the East-Central European region as a whole. Russia's real GDP growth rate, however, drastically slowed to 0.7 percent in 2014 from 4.1 percent in 2010. Some forecasts point to negative and low growth rates for the forthcoming years of 2016 and 2017. Russia's post-2016 GDP growth is projected to lag global and regional growth rates by two to three percentage points (more details can be found in Russia's growth outlook scenarios in Figure 2.2). Additionally, unfavorable forecasts for growth rates in fixed investments are likely to hamper Russia's future perspectives for economic development. To complicate macroeconomic growth, in addressing the issue of external debt (still manageable by international standards), Russia will be facing sizeable debt payment obligations and dwindling international reserves (Table 2.1). Future medium-term growth will be constrained

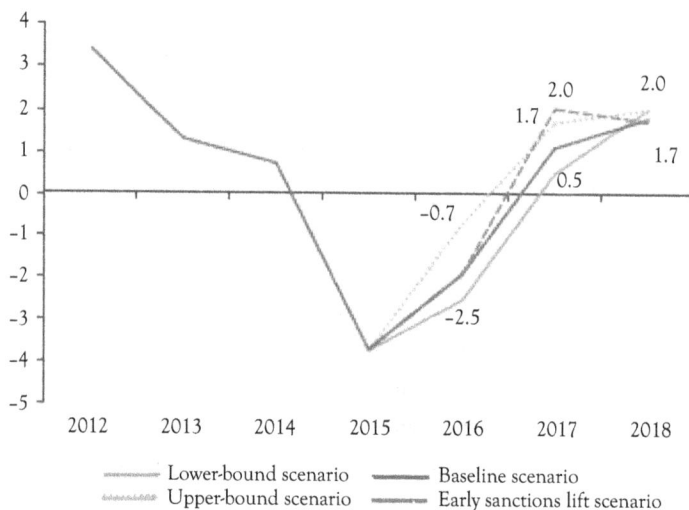

Figure 2.2 Real GDP growth projection, year-on-year, percent

Source: World Bank (2016b).

by commodity prices and ongoing economic sanctions, with the economic adjustment challenges now shifting to fiscal and financial sector restructuring as manufacturing growth constraints are noted as being high interest rates and high policy uncertainty (World Bank 2016b). The projections in Figure 2.2 reflect three possible oil price scenarios: the baseline, an upper-bound scenario and a lower-bound scenario. An alternative baseline scenario combines the baseline oil-price forecast with the projection assumption that economic sanctions would be lifted as early as 2017, while all other scenarios assume that economic sanctions would remain in place until 2018.

Market Attractiveness, Ease, Costs, and Risks of Doing Business

Market attractiveness, ease, costs, and risks of doing business vary across Russia's regions, markets, and industries. A general assessment of these strategic aspects of international corporate expansion can still be useful in the global country/market selection process. It can then be followed by a regional and sectorial strategic analysis.

According to the annual 2016 Market Potential Index (MPI) by globalEDGE, Russia's overall market attractiveness[3] ranked 35th out of the 87 countries included in the Index (1 being the most attractive and 87 being the least attractive). Russia's market size was ranked 18th, and its market growth rate 51st. Additional specifics on Russia's market potential can be found in Country Analysis Report—Russia (2014). Reflecting variations in market attractiveness across industries, Russia's overall MPI ranking in the Advanced Manufacturing Industry—taken as an example—was 48th. Its overall ranking in the Automotive Electronics and Composites/Lightweight Materials Industry MPI was 42nd out of 87 (globalEDGE 2016).

In addition to market attractiveness, country selection in global corporate expansion depends on low costs and the ease of doing business. Figures 2.3 and 2.4 profile Russia's global ranks on the ease of doing

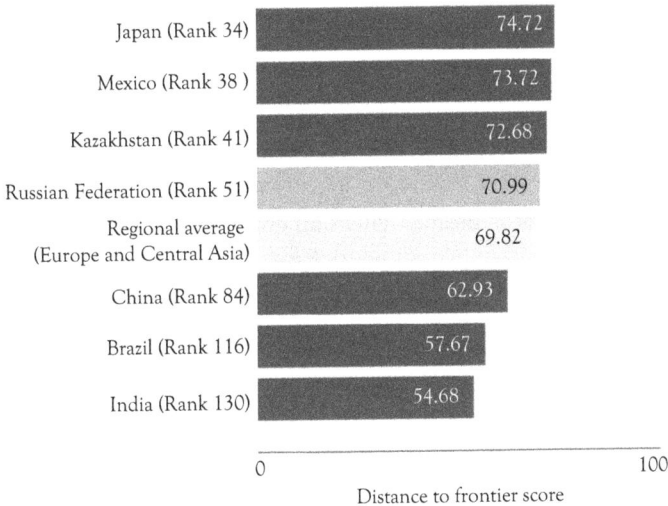

Japan (Rank 34)	74.72
Mexico (Rank 38)	73.72
Kazakhstan (Rank 41)	72.68
Russian Federation (Rank 51)	70.99
Regional average (Europe and Central Asia)	69.82
China (Rank 84)	62.93
Brazil (Rank 116)	57.67
India (Rank 130)	54.68

0   100

Distance to frontier score

Figure 2.3 Russia: Rankings on the ease of doing business compared to other economies

Source: World Bank (2016a).

[3] The overall country's market attractiveness in the weighted composite MPI Index is based on eight specific criteria: Market size, market intensity, market growth rate, market consumption capacity, commercial infrastructure, market receptivity, economic freedom, and country risk.

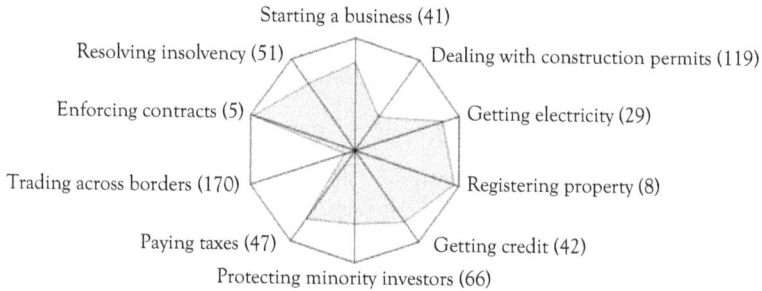

Starting a business (41)

Resolving insolvency (51)

Dealing with construction permits (119)

Enforcing contracts (5)

Getting electricity (29)

Trading across borders (170)

Registering property (8)

Paying taxes (47)

Getting credit (42)

Protecting minority investors (66)

Scale: Rank 189 center, rank 1 outer edge.

Figure 2.4 Russia: rankings on doing business across 10 specific business topics

Source: World Bank (2016).

business. These charts position Russia as superior compared to Brazil, China, and India, its BRIC counterparts. Russia also fares slightly better than the European region and Central Asia as a whole (Figure 2.3). The chart, presenting 10 specific topics of the ease of doing business framework in Russia (Figure 2.4), reveals some of the nation's relatively strong points, making it attractive for business (e.g., enforcing contracts and registering property) and weak in business environment (e.g., trading across borders, dealing with construction permits, and protecting minority investors). In addition to the rankings, the annual "Doing Business" report provides other valuable information on costs and procedures involved in doing business in the country. The ease/cost of performing business analysis can also be customized in a user-friendly side-by-side cross-country comparative format.

In their pursuit of high potential markets worldwide (typically characterized by large population and high GDP per capita) and premier global manufacturing locations (often characterized by availability of attractive factors of production and low cost of doing business as discussed earlier), corporations prefer stable patterns of socioeconomic development and growth.[4] Trading with or investing in a country with erratic patterns of development and growth raises unpredictability and risks that negatively affect business.

As Mark Twain said, it is difficult to make predictions, particularly about the future. Strategic risk assessment in international business tends to be a highly complex task. This complexity may be a result of large geographic distances, significant variations in political, economic, and legal systems, changes in government officials, and differences in cultural norms and business practices across the world. Possible risks in international business are strategic, operational, transactional, political, legal, technological, environmental, economic, financial, and can be caused by currency exchange, terrorism, planning, prices, customer satisfaction, mismanagement, competition, and various other factors.

---

[4] Numerous theories exist to explain and rationalize global patterns of foreign direct investment (FDI) across countries. FDI may be driven by Strategic Behavior caused by the rivalry in oligopolistic industries (industries composed of a limited number of large firms)—FDI flows reflect strategic rivalry between firms. This theory can be extended to Multipoint Competition (when two or more enterprises encounter each other in different regional markets, national markets, or industries). The Product Life Cycle theory argues that firms undertake FDI at particular stages in the life cycle of a product they have pioneered. Firms invest in other advanced countries when local demand in those countries grows large enough to support local production. Firms shift production to low-cost developing countries when product standardization and market saturation create price competition and cost pressures. The Eclectic Paradigm theory argues that in addition to the earlier factors, two additional factors must be considered when explaining both the rationale for and the direction of FDI: location-specific advantages that arise from using resource endowments or assets that are tied to a particular location and that a firm finds valuable to combine with its own unique assets and externalities—knowledge spillovers that occur when companies in the same industry locate in the same area (Hill and Hult 2016).

Some annual U.S. government publications on specific countries[5] offer excellent risk assessment information and analysis.[6] Over the years, leading global insurance companies have developed rigorous analytical methodological platforms and have published comprehensive country data that can be instrumental as sources of risk assessment information.

Russia's risk assessment by three leading global insurers is profiled in Figures 2.5 to 2.7. According to these profiles, doing business in Russia tends to fall in the medium risk range with elevated levels of risk for politics, government, and finance. Russia tends to present greater risks than the world average. This gap is particularly evident in the areas of International Transactions Policy and Business Environment risks.

In a broader context, the country's attractiveness, ease, costs, and risks of doing business can be also assessed in a composite form by analyzing country-specific sections in the annual Global Competitiveness Report (GCR) by the Swiss-based World Economic Forum. Figure 2.8 presents Russia's profile and categorizes the country as efficiency-driven, migrating toward the group of innovation-driven countries—the world's most advanced economies. As seen from Figure 2.8, Russia's overall global competitiveness rank improved against the previous year by eight positions. Russia's rankings in economic growth and competitiveness look superior to the neighboring Commonwealth of Independent States (countries of the former Soviet Union). Furthermore, across 12 "pillars of competitiveness" constituting the methodological framework of the GCR survey, Russia's relatively strong points include: large market size (ranked 6th out of 144 countries in the survey), macroeconomic environment (40th out of 144), and infrastructure (35th out of 144). Russia's weakest points lie

---

[5] For example: Country Commercial Guides by the U.S. Commercial Service www.export.gov/ccg, Investment Climate Statements by the U.S. Department of State http://www.state.gov/e/eb/rls/othr/ics/index.htm, National Trade Estimate Report on Foreign Trade Barriers by the U.S. Trade Representative https://ustr.gov/sites/default/files/2016-NTE-Report-FINAL.pdf.

[6] Browder (2015) provides an interesting and vivid personal account of business risks in Russia.

Export transactions

Political risk (1 to 7)

Short term

1 ▬▬▬▬▬▬▬▬▬▬▬▬▬ 7
        ▲

Medium/Long term

1 ▬▬▬▬▬▬▬▬▬▬▬▬▬ 7
          ▲

Special transactions

1 ▬▬▬▬▬▬▬▬▬▬▬▬▬ 7
        ▲

Commercial risk (A to C)

A ▬▬▬▬▬▬ B ▬▬▬▬▬▬ C
                    ▲

Direct investments (1 to 7)

War risk

1 ▬▬▬▬▬▬▬▬▬▬▬▬▬ 7
          ▲

Risk of expropriation and government action

1 ▬▬▬▬▬▬▬▬▬▬▬▬▬ 7
            ▲

Transfer risk

1 ▬▬▬▬▬▬▬▬▬▬▬▬▬ 7
          ▲

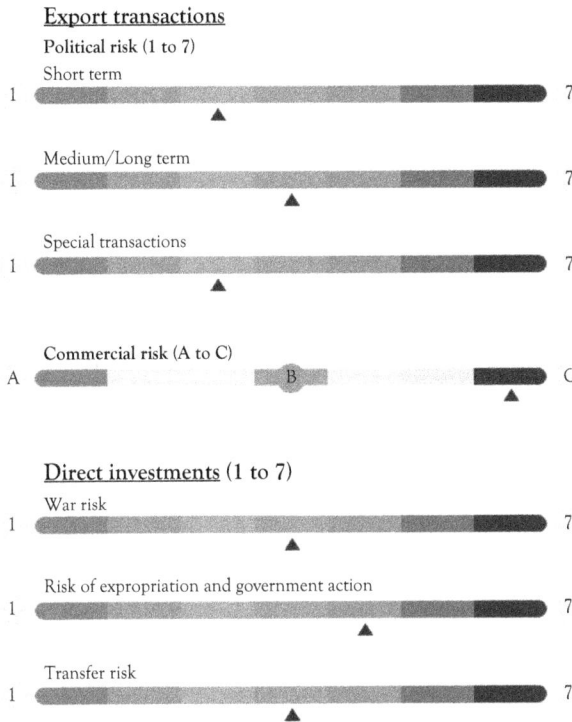

Figure 2.5 Russia: risk profile, Credendo Group/ONDD

Source: Credendo group/ONDD (2016).

Note: Level 1 on the 7-point scale signifies the lowest risk, level 7 signifies the highest risk. Level A in commercial risks signifies the lowest risk, level C signifies the highest risk.

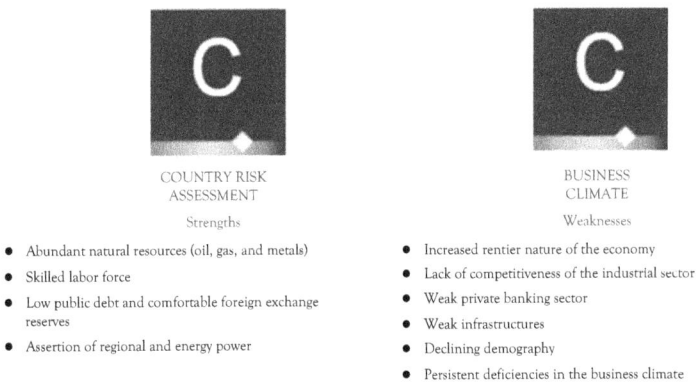

COUNTRY RISK
ASSESSMENT

BUSINESS
CLIMATE

Strengths

- Abundant natural resources (oil, gas, and metals)
- Skilled labor force
- Low public debt and comfortable foreign exchange reserves
- Assertion of regional and energy power

Weaknesses

- Increased rentier nature of the economy
- Lack of competitiveness of the industrial sector
- Weak private banking sector
- Weak infrastructures
- Declining demography
- Persistent deficiencies in the business climate

Figure 2.6(a) Russia: risk profile, Coface Group

Source: Coface (2016).

Economy to shrink again in 2016

- The recession in Russia is expected to continue but will be less severe in 2016. Private consumption, the main growth driver, is likely to remain constrained by a slower increase than in the past of nominal revenues, a relatively restrictive fiscal policy and the preference of households, notes at the beginning of the year, for deleveraging instead of consuming.
- Investment will remain limited by the lack of business owners' confidence, high interest rates, and by ongoing restrictions on financing in foreign currency imposed as part of Western sanctions. Budget constraints will limit the support for public investment. Spending increase in the hydrocarbon sector and defense may slow down.
- Inflation could slow, due to the strengthening of the ruble, but the consequences of the embargo placed on the purchase of certain products in Europe and Turkey may keep the prices of imported goods, especially food, relatively high.

Worsening fiscal and current account balance

- The fiscal deficit is expected to deepen in 2016. Low oil prices are likely to continue to put pressure on hydrocarbon revenues, while weak activity will curtail nonoil revenues. The draft 2016 budget includes a slow increase in pensions and a freeze on public sector wages. The defense budget is likely to continue to rise moderately. Comfortable foreign exchange reserves to cover this.
- The current account surplus is expected to stabilize in 2016. Exports, largely dominated by hydrocarbons are likely to remain constrained by low export prices. The weak competitiveness of Russian products could, moreover, limit nonoil exports, despite the fall of the ruble. However, depressed domestic demand, the maintenance of sanctions and embargos on certain European and Turkish products, should keep imports in check. FDIs are not likely to rebound in the absence of a real improvement in the situation in Ukraine and in governance.

Figure 2.6(b) Russia: risk profile, Coface Group

Source: Coface (2016).

in financial market development (95th out of 144), goods market efficiency (92nd out of 144), and institutions (100th out of 144) (Schwab 2015).[7]

---

[7] Since the publication of GCR 2015–2016, Russia's economy has continued deteriorating due to the weakening global energy prices (Russia's economy is critically dependent on oil and gas), poor performance of the domestic economy, and Western political-economic sanctions associated with the Russian-Ukrainian conflict and other causes.

- The stubbornly low oil price (to which the ruble exchange rate is strongly correlated) and due dates for external debt repayments are expected to maintain downward pressure on the ruble, the volatility of which has increased since the introduction of a floating exchange rate regime since the end of 2014. Russia's external debt (90 percent bank and business debt) is sharply lower and the high level of foreign exchange reserves limits the risks of default, without ruling this out for some businesses and banks. The banking sector's solvency and liquidity risk has increased significantly as a result of the worsening quality of the portfolio in a context not only of an economic crisis, but also the high cost of financing associated with the international sanctions that stop the major banks from accessing the financial markets.

A political situation expected to remain stable; persistent shortcomings in the business environment.

- Vladimir Putin's popularity nationally increased with the Russian intervention in Crimea in March 2014. Discontent within the population and the tensions could rise further in a context of economic downturn. The regime's increasingly tough stance reflected in the State's increased control of the media and the Internet, nonetheless significantly limits opposition movements' ability to organize and express themselves.
- Shortcomings relating to the protection of property rights, weak governance, and lack of corporate transparency significantly weaken the business environment. Despite some progress, Russia is ranked 168th (out of 215) on the World Bank's governance indicator, the corruption perceptions index, which is a recurrent weakness.

Figure 2.6(c) Russia: risk profile, Coface Group

Source: Coface (2016).

In a country as large and diverse as Russia, solely relying on the nationwide cost-efficiency-risk analysis is of limited practical value. There are significant variations in the nation's business environment that translate into differences in business benefits, costs, and risks across Russian regions and industries (to be discussed in the next chapters). A corporate analyst or a decision maker should bring these variations and differences in the big picture by conducting regional and local analyses. One way to accomplish this task is to engage U.S. Commercial Service

The Country Risk Tier (CRT) reflects A.M. Best's assessment of three categories of risk: Economic, Political and Financial System Risk.

• Russia, a CRT-4 country, has moderate levels of economic risk and high levels of political and financial system risk. While the country has economic potential due to its rich natural resources, strategic geographic and geopolitical position, and large well-educated work force it continues to be adversely impacted by materially lower oil and gas prices and economic sanctions.

• The country plays a significant political and economic role in the region and globally. It is expected that Russia will experience a second year of economic contraction. Gross domestic product in 2016 is forecasted at -1.8%, following the contraction in 2015 of -3.7%.

• The majority of countries pictured below are categorized as CRT-1 or CRT-2. Notable exceptions are the Eastern European countries of Bosnia and Herzegovina, Belarus and the Ukraine.

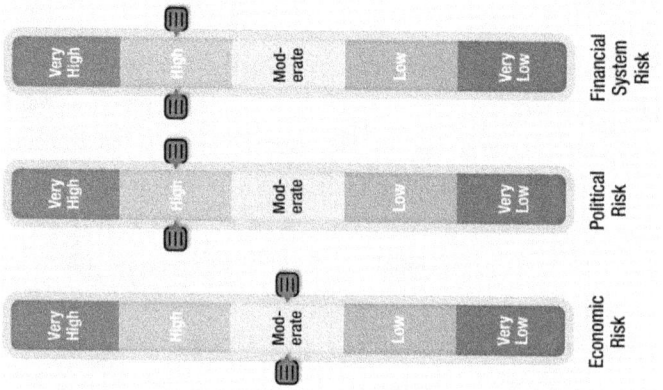

Political Risk Summary
Score 1 (best) to 5 (worst)

Source: A.M. Best

Figure 2.7(a) *Russia: risk profile, AM Best Rating & Criteria Center*

Source: AM Best (2016).

Political risk: High

- Russia has a highly centralized political system that is led by President Putin. Decision making lies with a narrow group of advisers within the presidential administration.
- The government will likely deal with increased civil protests due to challenging economic conditions. A devalued ruble, curtailed state spending and higher inflation for basic goods and services could increase government instability risks.
- The government is highly involved in economic activity, particularly in the energy sector. Continued intervention in the private sector has led to opaque regulations and an inefficient and corrupt legal system that suffers from political interference.
- Parliamentary elections are scheduled for December 2016. Presidential elections are schedule for March 2018. It is expected that Putin will run for a fourth term.
- Military involvement in numerous conflicts including the civil war in Syria, Ukraine's Crimean Peninsula, and conflicts resulting in sanctions with Egypt and Turkey have contributed to potential instability.

Figure 2.7(b) Russia: risk profile, AM Best Rating & Criteria Center

Source: AM Best (2016).

Financial system risk: High

- The Central Bank of Russia became the ultimate financial regulator for all financial institutions, including the insurance industry, in 2013. Operations for the Central Bank are carried out by its Financial Markets Service.
- Inflation continues to run above the Central Bank of Russia's target of 4.0 percent. Above target inflation is largely due to capital flight and a weaker ruble.
- There has been a reluctance of banks to make new loans, which will affect economic growth going forward. Banks have been shut out of international markets due to the ongoing sanctions. Nonperforming loans have increased from 11.5 percent at the beginning of 2015 to 14 percent at the end of 2015.

Figure 2.7(c) Russia: risk profile, AM Best Rating & Criteria Center

Source: AM Best (2016).

Key indicators, 2014

Population (millions)	143.7
GDP (US$ billions)	1,857.5
GDP per capita (US$)	12,926
GDP (PPP) as share (%) of world total	3.30

GDP (PPP) per capita (int'l $), 1990–2014

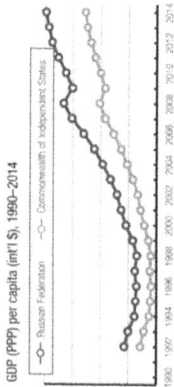

Global Competitiveness Index

	Rank (out of 140)	Score (1–7)
GCI 2015–2016	45	4.4
GCI 2014–2015 (out of 144)	53	4.4
GCI 2013–2014 (out of 148)	64	4.2
GCI 2012–2013 (out of 144)	67	4.2
Basic requirements (30.2%)	47	4.9
1st pillar: Institutions	100	3.5
2nd pillar: Infrastructure	35	4.8
3rd pillar: Macroeconomic environment	40	5.3
4th pillar: Health and primary education	56	5.9
Efficiency enhancers (50.0%)	40	4.5
5th pillar: Higher education and training	38	5.0
6th pillar: Goods market efficiency	92	4.2
7th pillar: Labor market efficiency	50	4.4
8th pillar: Financial market development	95	3.5
9th pillar: Technological readiness	60	4.2
10th pillar: Market size	6	5.9
Innovation and sophistication factors (19.8%)	76	3.5
11th pillar: Business sophistication	80	3.8
12th pillar: Innovation	68	3.3

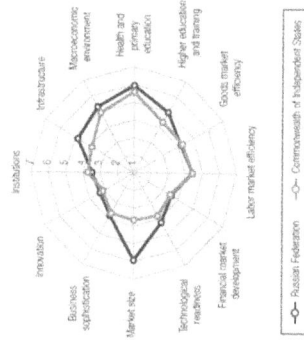

Stage of development

Figure 2.8 Russia: Global Competitiveness Index

Source: Schwab (2015).

in Russia (2016) and request their export assistance[8] designated for U.S. companies to identify and evaluate international partners, navigate international documentation challenges, create market entry strategies, and meet the challenges of selling in Russia. AmCham, American Chamber of Commerce in Russia (2016), can also be instrumental as a source of information, assistance, and business networking.

Leading Sectors for U.S. Exports and Investment

The latest U.S. Commercial Service's Country Commercial Guide 2016 Russia lists the following leading sectors for U.S. exports and investments in commercial sectors: Agricultural Equipment, Agricultural Sectors, Aviation Equipment, Broadcast Equipment, Building and Construction, Cosmetics and Perfumery, Food Processing and Packaging, Forestry and Woodworking, Franchising Industry, Machine Tools and Metal Working Equipment, Medical Equipment, Mining Equipment, Rail, Refinery Equipment, Safety and Security Equipment, and Water and Wastewater (U.S. Commercial Service 2016).

---

[8] U.S. Commercial Service in Russia offers U.S. business clients five major programs of assistance and support: (1) Gold Key Service—if the client would like to pursue the idea of exporting to Russia, but lacks the right connections, the Gold Key Service will connect it with Russian distributors, retailers or others who might be interested in its product. Gold Key Service includes prearranged face-to-face meetings for U.S. company representative and makes its time in Russia as productive as possible. (2) Platinum Key Service—is a customized, long-term support for larger U.S. companies looking to penetrate the Russian markets. (3) International Partner Search—the U.S. client will be connected with potential Russian business partners without even having to leave the U.S. (4) International Company Profile—this program involves a due diligence conducted on a company that the U.S. client might be interested in working with. And (5) Customized Business Facilitation Services—U.S. Commercial Service will help the U.S. client plan and host an event in Russia to introduce its product or promote its services. The events can be small info sessions, formal receptions, or large-scale networking events. U.S. Commercial Service in Russia can help book facilities, arrange catering, and most importantly, invite leading Russian businesspeople and government leaders in the client's industry to attend.

Medical Equipment

As an illustration, we included an excerpt from the U.S. Commercial Service's Country Commercial Guide 2016 Russia with the market analysis for the Medical Equipment sector in Russia.

Trends in the Medical Equipment Sector

A strong ruble devaluation and a cut in healthcare spending caused the Russian medical device market to experience further declines in 2015. Manufacturers of medical devices experienced tremendous reduction in sales of nearly 60 to 80 percent, which was partially compensated by growing demand for postsale services. Experts expect the Russian healthcare market to grow again, starting in 2017, induced by backlogged demand. Market insiders and market research experts recommend companies to keep sales channels open and carefully evaluate future setup. The post crisis market will be a different one. The health care system in Russia is reducing consumption of medical devices, including those domestically produced. According to market insiders, budget-allocated funding in 2015–2016 may be cut by 10 to 20 percent from the 2014 level, while the health care system still continues to be 80 to 85 percent dependent on imported products. Public consumers mostly request foreign medical devices, which increased in price by 30 to 40 percent due to the ruble devaluation.

According to the U.S. Commercial Service in Russia (Figure 2.9), after a drastic fall in 2013 Russia's medical device market in 2016–2018 is forecast to remain flat at 4.9 billion USD. The most important market barriers are: pessimistic forecasts on the general economic growth in the coming years; limited capacity of the regional budgets to finance expenditures on fixed assets for medical health facilities, due to the considerable pressure of social obligations in increase of salaries in the budget sphere; and termination of the regional healthcare modernization programs and the reduction of financing from the Federal budget.

Current changes in the regulatory framework increased uncertainty in the Russian market. They placed more pressure on foreign manufacturers

USD bln.

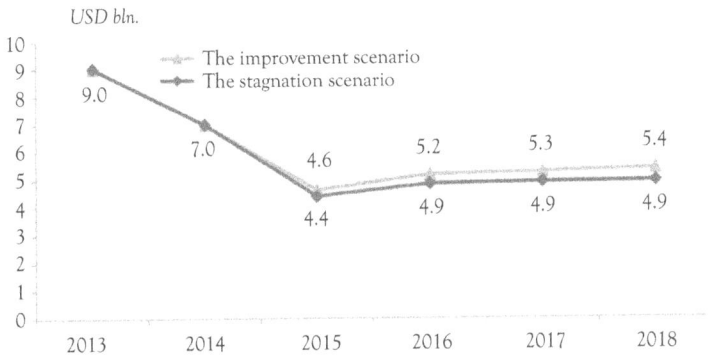

Figure 2.9 Forecast of Russian medical device market dynamics in 2015–2018, USD billion

Source: U.S. Commercial Service (2016).

and local distribution companies to evaluate and adapt their business models to the Russian market. Owing to the high government consumption share of the national medical device market—approximately 80 to 85 percent—there has been a clear government focus to foster further localization measures that have forced overseas medical device manufacturers to review their Russian business models. The Ministry of Industry and Trade of the Russian Federation approved in April 2015 a strategic five-year plan for import substitution in the pharmaceutical and medical device industry. Within this plan, there is a list of 111 groups of medical devices detailing targeted market shares of foreign manufacturers by 2020. Among them, for example, are surgical disposable materials (target is 40 percent imports in 2020, compared to 90 percent at the moment), prostheses, endoprostheses, and their parts, cardio pacemakers (10 percent import in 2020 vs. 85 percent now), endoscopes (35 percent vs. 100 percent), X-ray equipment, and other groups of medical devices. In February 2015, the Russian government published Act #102. This new legislation places limitations on how the Russian state and communities may purchase foreign medical devices. These limitations are part of the country's economic crisis recovery plan and cover about 40 different product categories, including CT and X-ray devices, ECG, and blood transfusion equipment.

The share of domestic medical products in the Russian market currently is about 15 percent. As of today, half of the 15 percent of medical products considered as domestic ones are still produced by foreign companies by the so-called "big four"—Philips, Siemens, General Electric, and Baxter. The level of localization varies from screwdriver assembly to more advanced production. However, the products have never reached 100 percent Russian content. About 4,400 companies are engaged in the production and maintenance of medical products in Russia. Market experts expect that in 2016–2017 domestically produced medical products will initiate a large-scale market penetration campaign.

The Russian public sector is the main user of medical products: approximately 85 percent of medical products are sold to state medical facilities. Private hospitals and patients represent the other 15 percent with purchases of primarily in vitro diagnostics, dentistry, and functional diagnostics (including ultrasound machines). A majority of polyclinics and primary care facilities as well as some diagnostic centers and hospitals are controlled by the municipal administration.

The federal administration controls research institutes, clinical activity of the Russian Academy of Medical Sciences, research centers, and medical training organizations. Federal medical facilities account for about 4 percent of the total bed capacity in Russia. In addition, there are other special organizations—institutional medical establishments in Russia, which are under the patronage of such organizations as federal ministries or Russian Railways, for instance. This segment is estimated at about 15 percent of out-patient and 6 percent of in-patient facilities. The private segment is concentrated in mainly urban areas and in out-patient services, typically in certain specialties such as dental clinics. Clients of such private and privileged facilities are mostly wealthy Russians and foreign expats. In Russia, the ownership of the medical organization is not necessarily connected to the source of funds. Federal, regional, municipal, and institutional clinics and hospitals may easily offer paid services to the public, while private clinics may participate in the OMS (Obligatory Medical Insurance) system and be funded by it. The per capita availability of basic medical equipment in Russia is three to five times lower than in developed countries. Medical organizations at the federal and institutional level as a rule have a wide range of modern medical equipment, but in case of regional, and especially municipal hospitals and clinics, medical equipment is often outdated and does not correspond to the needs of the institutions. For high-technology medical devices such as equipment for diagnostics of cancer, the situation is even worse, as Russia has 15 times fewer of these devices than Western countries. Geographically speaking, the more remote a hospital is, the worse it is equipped. Private clinics usually have state-of-the-art equipment because this is one of their main marketing attractions. Even if medical clinics and hospitals are equipped with modern equipment, lack of training for the medical personnel and missing repair work might be reasons why the equipment cannot be used as planned. Information on the funding of the healthcare sector and the structure of public procurement in medical equipment in Russia by device category are provided in Figures 2.10 and 2.11.

U.S. Commercial Service in Russia reports that the registration of medical devices and medical equipment in Russia is challenging. On February 2015, the Russian government implemented restrictions for admission to state tenders for certain types of medical devices. This measure was taken as a part of the initiative supporting the import substitution program and promoting the development of domestic manufacturing of medical devices. According to the published Decree #102, which contains a list of certain types of medical devices (45 items) originating from foreign countries subject to restrictions for state and municipal procurements in the Russian Federation. Foreign manufacturers' participation in state and municipal tenders will be denied if there are two or more entries from Russia Belarus, Armenia, and Kazakhstan. The Eurasian Economic Commission (EEC)[9] is currently developing subordinate acts to implement the strategic agreement on common principles and rules of circulation

---

[9] The Eurasian Economic Union (EAEU or EEU) is an economic union of five states located primarily in northern Eurasia. A treaty aiming for the establishment of the EEU was signed in May 2014 by the leaders of Belarus, Kazakhstan, and Russia, and came into force on January 1, 2015. Treaties aiming for Armenia's and Kyrgyzstan's accession to the EEU were signed in October 2014 and December 2014, respectively. Armenia's accession treaty came into force on January 2, 2015. Kyrgyzstan's accession treaty came into effect in August 2015. Russia plays a dominant political-economic in the EAEU.

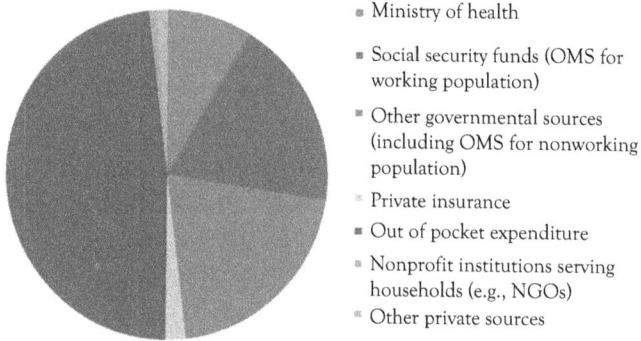

- Ministry of health
- Social security funds (OMS for working population)
- Other governmental sources (including OMS for nonworking population)
- Private insurance
- Out of pocket expenditure
- Nonprofit institutions serving households (e.g., NGOs)
- Other private sources

Figure 2.10 Funding of the healthcare sector in Russia, 2013

Source: U.S. Commercial Service (2016).

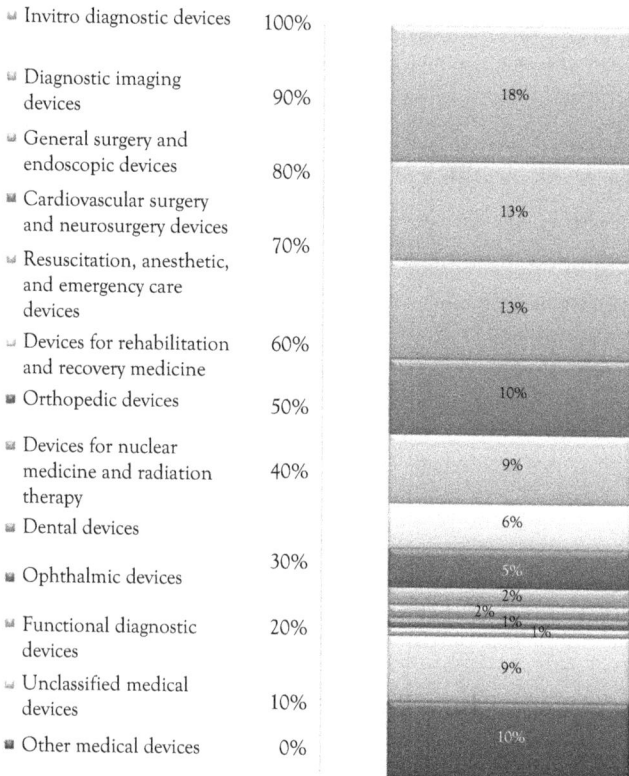

- Invitro diagnostic devices
- Diagnostic imaging devices
- General surgery and endoscopic devices
- Cardiovascular surgery and neurosurgery devices
- Resuscitation, anesthetic, and emergency care devices
- Devices for rehabilitation and recovery medicine
- Orthopedic devices
- Devices for nuclear medicine and radiation therapy
- Dental devices
- Ophthalmic devices
- Functional diagnostic devices
- Unclassified medical devices
- Other medical devices

Figure 2.11 The structure of public procurement in Russia by device category

Source: U.S. Commercial Service (2016).

for medical devices in the Eurasian economic space signed in December 2014. More than 10 legal acts addressing medical devices were expected in 2015, but for the moment, only one of them (Guidelines to define a safety class for medical and in-vitro devices) has been agreed upon and accepted. The list of Essential Principles of Safety and Performance of Medical Devices and common marking, labeling, and testing requirements are currently under discussion and may be agreed upon and published in the near future. Meanwhile, the EEC has been consistent in their message that the new system will go into effect in the first half of 2016 and replace current national regulations. At the beginning of 2015, Russia implemented amendments to the civil and penal codes and significantly increased penalties for the manufacturing, sale, or trade of counterfeit and unregistered pharmaceuticals and medical devices in accordance with the MEDICRIME European convention signed in 2011.

Subsector Best Prospects

Despite recent breakthroughs and the fact that locally produced medical equipment is two to four times cheaper than imported equipment, Russian production still lags behind the majority of developed countries. Russia is still heavily dependent on imports for a significant number of the medical equipment industry subsectors, especially those requiring large investments in research and development (R&D), innovative technologies, and automation. The most promising market segments include diagnostics and visualization, cardiovascular, ophthalmology, orthopedics, laboratory diagnostics, and urology equipment and technology. In the Russian market product mix, pricing and service offerings should be flexible toward changing customer preferences and a growing competitive environment.

Opportunities

The broad scale of the healthcare industry development in Russia drives the demands for highly innovative materials, devices, and technologies that do not yet have substitutes on the Russian market. This creates various opportunities for the U.S. companies working in this sector. The federal government's order #2302 of September 12, 2013 requires construction and commissioning of 32 perinatal centers. Most of these projects will start late in 2016—early in 2017. In 2015–2017, measures to develop nuclear medicine should come into effect, creating some demand for new devices. The actual support for localization of production of pharmaceutical products and medical devices in Russia could open business opportunities for U.S. suppliers of these industries. The bulk of imports are in the segments of diagnostic imaging devices, In vitro diagnostic devices and general surgery and endoscopic devices (Figure 2.11).

References

AM Best. August 24, 2016. "Russia." www3.ambest.com/ratings/cr/reports/russia.pdf

Browder, B. 2015. *Red Notice: A True Story of High Finance, Murder, and One Man's Fight for Justice.* New York: Simon & Schuster.

Central Intelligence Agency. 2016. *The World Factbook 2016.* Washington, DC: Central Intelligence Agency. www.cia.gov/library/publications/the-world-factbook/geos/rs.html

Coface. July 2016. /www.coface.com/Economic-Studies-and-Country-Risks/Russian-Federation

"Country Analysis Report—Russia—In-depth PESTLE Insights." 2014. Marketline. www.marketresearch.com/MarketLine-v3883/Country-Russia-PESTLE-Insights-8644418/

Economist Intelligence Unit. 2015. *Country Report. Russia,* p. 29. http://country.eiu.com/russia

Economist Intelligence Unit. September 2016. *Country Report. Russia.*

Economist Intelligence Unit. 2016a. *Country Report. Brazil,* p. 11. http://country.eiu.com/russia

Economist Intelligence Unit. 2016b. *Country Report. China,* p. 10. http://country.eiu.com/china.

Economist Intelligence Unit. 2016c. *Country Report. Germany,* p. 11 http://country.eiu.com/germany.

Economist Intelligence Unit. 2016d. *Country Report. India,* p. 11 http://country.eiu.com/india.

Economist Intelligence Unit. 2016e. *Country Report. Russia,* p. 11. http://country.eiu.com/russia

globalEDGE. 2016. "Market Potential Index." http://globaledge.msu.edu/mpi (accessed September 3, 2016).

Grimes, W. 2015. "To Russia with Capitalist Ambitions." *New York Times*, Feb 2.

Helliwell, J.F., R. Layard, and J. Sachs, eds. 2016. *World Happiness Report 2016 Update*. New York: Sustainable Development Solutions Network.

Hill, C., and T. Hult. 2016. *Global Business Today*. 9th ed. New York, NY: McGrawHill/Irvin.

Hsu, A. 2016. *The 2016 Environmental Performance Index*. New Haven, CT: Yale Center for Environmental Law and Policy.

Human Development Report. 2015. *Work for Human Development*. New York, NY: United Nations Development Programme. http://hdr.undp.org/sites/all/themes/hdr_theme/country-notes/RUS.pdf

Russia Economic Report. Policy Uncertainty Clouds Medium-Term Prospects. 2014.

Schwab, K. 2015. *The Global Competitiveness Report 2015–2016*. Geneva: World Economic Forum. www3.weforum.org/docs/gcr/2015-2016/Global_Competitiveness_Report_2015-2016.pdf

"The World Bank in the Russian Federation." September 2014. http://documents.worldbank.org/curated/en/169891468306528030/pdf/912390WP0WB0RE00Box385330B00PUBLIC0.pdf

U.S. Commercial Service. 2016. "Doing Business in Russia: 2016 Country Commercial Guide for U.S. Companies." https://www.export.gov/article?id=Russia-market-overview.

U.S. Department of State. 2015. "Investment Climate Statement—Russia." www.state.gov/e/eb/rls/othr/ics/investmentclimatestatements/index.htm?year=2016&dlid=254409

World Bank. 2016a. "Doing Business 2016." Measuring Regulatory Quality and Efficiency. Economy Profile: Russian Federation. www.doingbusiness.org/data/exploreeconomies/~/media/giawb/doing%20business/documents/profiles/country/RUS.pdf?ver=3

World Bank. 2016b. "The Long Journey to Recovery" *Russia Economic Report*, no. 35, pp. 1–78. http://documents.worldbank.org/curated/en/657991467989516696/pdf/104825-NWP-P156290-PUBLIC-WB-RER-No-35-FINAL-ENG.pdf.

Zhuplev, A. 2008. "Economic Internationalization of Russia: Roots, Trends, and Scenarios." *International Political Science Review* 29, no. 1, pp. 99–119.

CHAPTER 3

Russia's Main Industries and Their Attractiveness for International Business

While Russians have shown huge strength and resilience in standing up again and again after being knocked down, the big question for me is how can Russians in future stop being knocked down? Instead of focusing energy and attention on getting up again after yet another blow, how can Russia be mere pro-active and not get knocked down in the first place?

—David Steer
President and General Director, Kraft Foods Russia

Main Points in This Chapter

- Industry structure.
- Main industries, their profiles, trends, and business attractiveness.
- Consumer trends and marketing strategies.

Industry Structure

According to the Global Economic Forum classification, Russia belongs to the group of 20 economies transitioning from efficiency-driven to inno- vation driven, stage 3 category. Its position is in the middle of the Global Economic Forum classification's spectrum, ranging from factor-driven economies—in essence, less developed economies—to innovation-driven economies—in essence, highly developed economies (Schwab 2015).

As of 2016, Russian GDP had the following structural economic composition by sector of origin: agriculture—4.4 percent, industry—35.8 percent, and services—59.7 percent (The World Factbook 2016). Within services—Russia's largest economic sector—the leading segments are wholesale and retail trade, repair of motor vehicles, motorcycles, and personal and household goods (together totaling 17 percent of the nation's GDP), public administration, real estate, renting, and business activities (totaling 12 percent), transport and communications (totaling 9 percent), and education, health, and social work (totaling 7 percent) (Russia' 2015 Statistical Pocketbook 2015). From an international business viewpoint, services, compared to industrial goods, tend to have different dynamics and unique challenges and therefore require different approaches.[1] Passport estimates that 5.9 percent of the Russian work force is employed in agriculture. Although the soil is fertile, years of neglect have led to yields that are just a third of those in Western Europe. Farmers are ill-prepared to meet the goal of self-sufficiency that officials have abruptly imposed in response to Western sanctions. For example, up to half of the fruit production from small farms and 20 percent of industrial vegetable production is lost to spoilage each year (Russia: Country Profile 2016).

According to Passport, Russia's manufacturing sector accounts for 14.4 percent of GDP and employs 13.2 percent of the work force. Several

---

[1] Services can be crucial in stimulating goods exports and are critical in maintaining those transactions. Many U.S. merchandise exports would not take place if they were not supported by such service activities as banking, insurance, and transportation. The many obvious differences between services and products include differences in tangibility and customer involvement. Since services are intangible, communicating a service offer is more difficult than communicating a product offer. Also, services must be frequently tailored to the specific needs of the client. Such adaptation often necessitates the client's direct participation and cooperation. Involving the client, in turn, calls for interpersonal skills and cultural sensitivity on the part of the service provider. The intangibility of services makes financing somewhat more difficult—given that no form of collateral is involved—and financial institutions may be less willing to provide financial support to your company. However, many public and private institutions will provide financial assistance to creditworthy service exporters (U.S. Commercial Service 2015a).

international automobile firms operate production facilities in Russia but the industry has been hit hard by sanctions. Car sales dropped by approximately one-third in 2015. The food and chemical industry is gaining market share after Russia restricted Western imports but many industries are struggling. Investment in manufacturing has been anemic, but in 2015 Moscow and Beijing agreed to a slew of loans and investments totaling U.S.$25 billion which will help cushion the impact of Western sanctions. The real value of gross manufacturing value added fell by 0.1 percent in 2014 but declined much more rapidly in the first half of 2015.

There are massive mineral and forest resources with iron ore, coal, copper, aluminum, manganese, salt, and precious metals all being produced, though facilities are in need of modernization. Raw materials, such as oil, natural gas, and metals make up more than two-thirds of all export revenues. South Korean, Japanese, and Chinese investors hope to move into the Russian market to secure stable supplies of coal and other energy resources. Mining output grew by 4.3 percent in real terms during 2015.

Services make up 61.8 percent of GDP. Just two large banks (Sberbank and VTB) dominate the Russian banking market with 60 to 70 percent of deposits. Unsecured credit growth poses an increasing financial risk. Retail sales have fallen steadily in 2016, with an overall 10 percent fall in 2015. The real value of tourist receipts rose by 6.9 percent in 2015, however, and a gain of 1.8 percent is forecast for 2016 (Russia: Country Profile 2016). Within industry, Russia's second largest economic sector after services is manufacturing; it comprises 15 percent of the total Russian GDP. Mining/quarrying and construction, the most important industry segments, contribute 10 and 7 percent, respectively, to the GDP (Federal State Statistics Service 2015). Russia has a range of mining and extractive industries producing coal, oil, gas, chemicals, and metals; all forms of machine building from rolling mills to high-performance aircraft and space vehicles; defense industries (including radar, missile production, advanced electronic components), shipbuilding; road and rail transportation equipment; communications equipment; agricultural machinery, tractors, and construction equipment; electric power generating and transmitting equipment; medical and scientific instruments; consumer durables, textiles, foodstuffs, and handicrafts. In 2015, Russia's industrial production growth rate declined to 3.5 percent. In contrast, in 2012 Russia's labor force (75.25 million, or 52.8 percent of the total population) composition was as follows: agriculture—9.7 percent, industry—27.8 percent, and services— 62.5 percent (The World Factbook 2016). Table 3.1 contrasts the origins of Russian GDP with that of its fellow BRICS and "inspirational comparators," Germany and the United States. In this comparison, Russia looks less reliant on agriculture compared to other BRICS, but its agricultural GDP share is significantly higher than that of Germany and the United States. Russia's industrial share in GDP is lower than that of China, but still considerably higher than in both its BRICS peers and "inspirational comparators." Accordingly, while Russia's share of services in GDP trails that of Brazil, Germany, South Africa, and the United States, it is slightly higher than India's and considerably higher than China's.

The big picture and internal sectorial dynamics in Russian agriculture, industry, and services highlight the industry's paramount economic role as well as its relatively higher efficiency and global competitiveness in contrast to the agricultural and service sectors.

The reader interested in a broader retrospective understanding can derive a comprehensive review of Russia from the U.S. Library of Congress' Russian Country Study. This review covers the country's

Table 3.1 Russia versus BRICS and "aspirational comparators": *GDP origins, percent share*

	GDP origins		
	Agriculture	Industry	Services
Brazil	5.9	22.2	71.9
China	8.9	42.7	48.4
Germany	0.7	30.2	69.1
India	16.1	29.5	54.4
Russia	4.4	35.8	59.7
South Africa	2.4	30.3	67.4
United States	1.6	20.8	77.6

Source: The World Factbook (2016).

economic and industrial development in terms of historical setting, geography, society, economy, political system, and foreign policy (Curtis 1998). A Harvard sponsored comparative study conducted in the late 1980s provides unique political-economic insights on the U.S.S.R. as well as transitional Russia under Gorbachev (Lawrence and Vlachoutsicos 1990). The Gaidar Institute for Economic Policy (Gaidar Institute) publishes a range of up-to-date annual, monthly, and special analytical reports. The Institute's annual "Russian Economy Trends and Outlooks" report delivers comprehensive, analytical coverage of such topics as sociopolitical context, the monetary and budgetary sector, financial markets and financial institutions, the real sector of the economy, the social sphere, and institutional problems (Российская экономика в 2014 году 2015). Specific information on Russian accounting practices, taxation, customs duties, currency controls, and other regulatory issues can be obtained from Deloitte (Deloitte 2015). Russian government agencies and numerous international institutions and organizations also publish a wide selection of macroeconomic reports on Russia—the "Sources of Information" section of this book provides more detail.

International business investors or corporate strategists, contemplating expansion to Russia, should keep in mind that although some Russian industries may appear attractive on the basis of their economic size and market potential, there are administrative barriers and other noneconomic factors that can make strategic entry into these industries costly, logistically complicated and even impossible. Entry and operational impediments include burdensome regulatory regimes, inadequate intellectual property rights, protection and enforcement, widespread corruption and inadequate rule of law, inconsistent application of laws and regulations, lack of transparency, and a nonlevel playing field for competition due to the continued presence of large state-owned or state-controlled enterprises dominating strategic sectors of the economy. Investments in the wide-ranging and ever-changing list of "strategic sectors" of the Russian economy are subject to Russian Government control (U.S. Commercial Service 2016; U.S. Department of State 2016).

Main Industries, Their Profiles, Trends, and Business Attractiveness

The Russian economy is dominated by large, often government-owned and government-controlled corporations.[2] The small and medium enterprises (SMEs) segment plays a relatively minor role (Chapter 5 provides additional illustrations of Russian SMEs). Reflective of Russia's general macroeconomic trends, the national economy and its industry sector remain highly dependent on mining, extraction, and low value-added manufacturing. According to the latest Forbes' 2000 Global Index, 10 out of 27 of Russia's largest public corporations represent the Energy sector (mostly oil and gas), 6 operate in the Mining, Minerals, and Metals sector, 5 companies represent Financial Services, 2 are in Retail, 1 is in Chemicals, and 1 is in the Technology sector (globalEDGE 2016). Our further discussion in this chapter will focus on the energy sector, the backbone of the Russian economy. We will discuss the energy sector's role in the national economy, drivers, trends, and developmental dynamics from a general strategic perspective. This will be followed by several Russian industries potentially attractive in the international marketing context.

Energy Sector

As a country of vast geography and geopolitical aspirations, richly endowed in mineral resources, Russia is a premier global energy power. The nation enjoys top global rankings in energy; it holds number 2 in natural gas production and consumption, 1 in natural gas exports and proved reserves, 3 in crude oil production, 2 in crude oil exports, 8 in proved crude oil reserves, 4 in electricity production, and 25 in electricity exports (The World Factbook 2016). Russia is the third-largest generator of nuclear power in the world and fourth-largest in terms of installed nuclear capacity. With nine nuclear reactors currently under construction, Russia is the second country in the world, after China, in terms of

---

[2] The 2016 annual Index of Economic Freedom by the Heritage Foundation places Russia in the "mostly unfree" category, ranking it 153rd out of 178 countries worldwide. Russia is also ranked 41st out of 43 countries in the European region (Index of Economic Freedom 2016).

number of reactors under construction as of March 2015 (U.S. Department of Energy 2015).

Historically, energy and commodities—particularly oil, natural gas, metals, and timber—have played critical roles in Russia's domestic and foreign political-economic agenda. Illustratively, in 2014 the product composition of Russian principal exports was as follows: oil fuel and gas—70.5 percent of the total, metals—10.5 percent, chemicals—5.9 percent, machinery and equipment—5.3 percent, and other items—7.8 percent (Country Report: Russia 2016). The combined oil and gas revenues account for more than 50 percent of the federal budget revenues (U.S. Department of Energy 2015). In contrast, Russia's position in renewable energy is weak; its worldwide rankings are low and the volumes and shares in the overall energy balance are tiny (Table 3.2).

The advent of the Industrial Revolution and proliferation of oil as a major fuel worldwide in the late 19th to early 20th century have amplified this pattern. Over the past few decades, under the U.S.S.R. and post-U.S.S.R., Russia has become extraordinarily dependent on high world oil prices and energy exports. After the dissolution of the U.S.S.R., Russia embarked on the mission to regain its lost status as a super power. In fulfilling this mission, the nation has been heavily relying on energy as strategic leverage in its political pursuits, as global oil prices have skyrocketed over the past decade before global energy prices took a steep plunge in 2014, creating a strong downward trend prevalent today (Figure 3.1).

Russia's energy sector[3] plays a supreme political-economic role; this sector alone makes up 27 percent of the national GDP, employs 3.5 percent of labor, constitutes 70 percent of total exports, and generates 53 percent of overall tax proceeds (Итоги работы Минэнерго России 2015). Far beyond macroeconomics, Russia's highly centralized political system, sheer military power inherited from the U.S.S.R., and historically dominant role in Eurasia—especially in the "near abroad"—altogether explain the extraordinary significance of the energy sector in the Russian

---

[3] Russian government documents, scholarly publications, and mass media often use the term "топливно-энергетический комплекс" (the fuel-energy complex)—a complex of industries that operate in the extraction, processing, and transportation of fuel, as well as electricity generation.

Table 3.2 *Russian energy sector: Retrospect and projections*

| | Russia | | | | | | Comparisons CAAGR 2010–2035, percent | | |
| | Energy demand, Mtoe* | | | | Shares, percent | | | | |
	1990	2010	2025	2035	2010	2035	Russia	OECD Europe	China
Total primary energy demand	880	710	802	875	100	100	0.8	0.0	1.9
Coal	191	115	122	128	16	15	0.4	-2.0	0.8
Oil	264	139	163	168	20	19	0.7	-1.0	2.1
Gas	367	389	420	454	55	52	0.6	0.6	6.6
Nuclear	31	45	64	74	6	8	2.0	-0.5	10.9
Hydro	14	14	17	20	2	2	1.4	0.6	2.6
Bioenergy	12	7	10	18	2	2	3.9	2.3	0.4
Other renewables	0	0	7	15	0	2	15.2	6.2	9.0
Power generation	444	372	406	443	100	100	0.7	0.2	2.8
Coal	105	71	77	85	19	19	0.7	-2.7	1.5
Oil	62	11	8	7	3	2	-2.0	-4.9	-1.9
Gas	228	226	225	229	61	52	0.1	1.0	8.2
Nuclear	31	45	64	74	12	17	2.0	-0.5	10.9
Hydro	14	14	17	20	4	5	1.4	0.6	2.6
Bioenergy	4	4	7	14	1	3	4.6	2.2	12.4

Other renewables	0	0	7	15	0	3	15.2	6.5	13.8
Other energy sector	127	120	125	131	21	26	0.3	-0.6	0.7
Electricity	21	25	29	34	100	100	1.2	-0.2	2.5
Total final consumption	625	448	523	570	100	100	1.0	0.2	1.9
Coal	55	19	20	20	4	3	0.1	-0.8	-0.3
Oil	145	104	129	139	23	24	1.2	-0.9	2.6
Gas	143	146	174	197	32	35	1.2	0.5	6.4
Electricity	71	62	80	92	14	16	1.6	0.8	3.6
Heat	203	115	117	119	26	21	0.1	0.7	0.6
Bioenergy	8	2	3	4	1	1	2.0	2.4	-1.6
Other renewables	—	—	0	0	—	0	n.a.	5.4	4.3
Industry	209	132	147	163	100	100	0.8	0.3	1.7
Coal	15	15	16	16	11	10	0.3	-0.3	-0.2
Oil	25	11	14	17	8	10	1.6	-1.2	1.1
Gas	30	33	37	43	25	27	1.1	0.2	8.3
Electricity	41	28	36	41	21	25	1.6	0.6	3.4
Heat	98	45	44	44	34	27	-0.0	0.1	0.4
Bioenergy	—	0	1	1	0	0	3.0	0.1	n.a.
Other renewables	—	—	—	—	—	—	n.a.	6.5	3.3
Transport	116	97	122	131	100	100	1.2	-0.4	4.2

(Continued)

Table 3.2 Russian energy sector: Retrospect and projections   (Continued)

| | Russia | | | | | | Comparisons CAAGR 2010–2035, percent | | |
| | Energy demand, Mtoe* | | | | Shares, percent | | Russia | OECD Europe | China |
	1990	2010	2025	2035	2010	2035			
Oil	73	56	74	77	58	59	1.2	-0.9	4.1
Electricity	9	7	9	12	8	9	1.9	2.3	7.0
Biofuels	—	—	—	—	—	—	n.a.	4.1	12.4
Other fuels	34	33	39	42	34	32	0.9	3.2	1.6
Buildings	228	149	169	178	100	100	0.7	0.6	1.0
Coal	40	4	4	3	3	2	-1.1	-1.9	-1.8
Oil	12	6	5	5	4	3	-1.3	-1.7	-0.9
Gas	57	44	55	61	30	34	1.3	0.6	6.2
Electricity	15	26	32	35	17	20	1.3	0.9	4.2
Heat	98	67	70	71	45	40	0.2	1.0	0.9
Bioenergy	7	2	2	3	1	1	1.5	1.8	-2.3
Other renewables	—	—	0	0	—	0	n.a.	5.4	4.4
Other	72	70	86	99	100	100	1.4	-0.2	1.2

Source: Compiled from World Energy Outlook. New Policies Scenario, (2012, 570, 592, 600).
Note: *Mtoe: Million tons of oil equivalents.

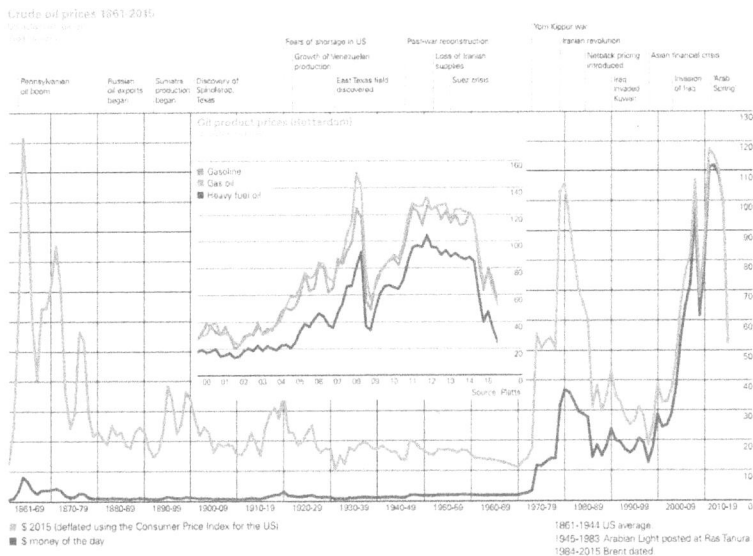

Figure 3.1 Crude Oil Prices 1861–2014, U.S. dollars per barrel;
World Events

Source: BP, Statistical Review of World Energy (2015, 14, 15).

national identity, domestic and foreign policy, as well as inner power dynamics and politics (Zhuplev and Shtykhno 2015).

MarketLine, a consultancy, reports that the Russian oil and gas market growth rate has plummeted in value lately from its peak of 33.5 percent in 2011 to negative 1 percent in 2014 (the volume growth numbers are 2.9 percent and 0.7 percent, respectively). MarketLine forecasts the 2019 oil and gas market growth rate at negative 0.9 percent in value and 1.0 percent in volume growth (Oil & Gas in Russia 2014). Figure 3.2, drawing on the Porter's "diamond" model, profiles the competitive picture in the Russian oil and gas industry on a scale of 1 (weakest) to 5 (strongest) and provides detailed strategic and financial analysis of the four Russian leading oil and gas companies.

In line with industry trends worldwide, Russia's leading oil and gas companies are large, integrated players that benefit from the scale of their operations. The presence of such incumbents intensifies rivalry in the market. The oil industry is divided into two main segments: upstream and downstream. The upstream segment includes activities such as

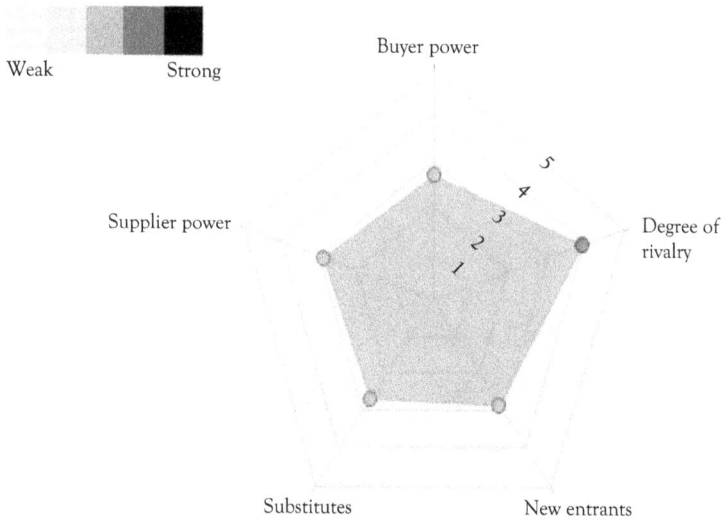

Figure 3.2 *Forces driving competition in the oil and gas industry in Russia, 2014*

Source: Oil and Gas in Russia (2014, 13).

exploration and exploitation of oil and natural gas, while the downstream segment includes activities such as refining and distribution of petroleum products in the form of fuel, heating oil, or raw material for the petrochemical industry. Oil companies may specialize in a specific segment or do business in both these segments. The Russian oil and gas market is dominated by large, diversified international companies with highly vertically integrated operations throughout oil exploration, production, refining, transportation, and marketing (Russia's Transneft, however, holds a monopoly over Russia's pipeline network). Both the presence of these powerful incumbents and the need for substantial initial investment to set up facilities such as drilling rigs reduce the threat of new companies establishing themselves in this market. In 2008, the market experienced increased demand for specialist equipment and services as commodity prices went sky high, pushing drilling companies to explore commodities deposits previously deemed too costly, and boosting suppliers' revenues. This trend eventually stopped and saw commodity prices fall drastically around 2009. However, 2010 saw the price of commodities starting to recover, resulting in strong market growth for 2010 and 2011. This level of healthy growth ceased in 2012 when market value growth decelerated, with 2013 showing marginal decline and a similar story anticipated for 2014. Substitutes in the oil and gas market can be considered in terms of increasing the production of alternative energy sources, although this can also result in high switching costs. High fixed costs and exit barriers intensify the competition level within the market (Oil & Gas in Russia 2014).

The Economist Intelligence Unit's country report forecasts that Russia's near-term energy output growth will remain sluggish, with oil companies struggling to increase production as existing fields are depleted and recovery becomes more difficult. According to this report, production in Western Siberia peaked some years ago. Russia is running out of cheap oil, as the "legacy" assets inherited from the Soviet Union begin to decline. The remaining oil is deeper, harder to access, and less profitable because of higher production costs. To prevent declining production, the industry will have to expand to more remote and geologically complex areas, such as the Arctic offshore. The share of fixed investment in GDP is lower than in many emerging markets. Impediments to faster growth include the economy's high and growing dependence on natural-resource sectors and manifold institutional weaknesses (in particular, high corruption). Additionally, conventional wisdom that Russia is well endowed with human capital looks out-of-date. Russia shows up poorly in international comparisons for mathematics and science. Cross-country evidence confirms that, on average, Russian companies are poorly managed. Medium-term growth will also be constrained by the exceptionally low level of entrepreneurship (Country Report: Russia 2015; Global Entrepreneurship Monitor 2016). This is reflected in the oil industry dynamics (Figure 3.3); as is evident, growth in oil reserves is slowing down, capital investment is increasing, production output is flat, and exports fluctuate between stagnation and decline.

Dynamics for the Russian natural gas industry presented in Figure 3.4 reveal similar trends: stagnant/declining capital investment, flat production output, and stagnant domestic supply and exports. The Scenarios for Russian Federation report by the World Economic Forum (2013) highlights three strategic challenges stemming from the changing global energy landscape that Russia will face in the coming decades: increased supplies of oil from "new" sources ranging from the United States to Iraq; threat of unconventional gas resources given the potential of shale to undermine

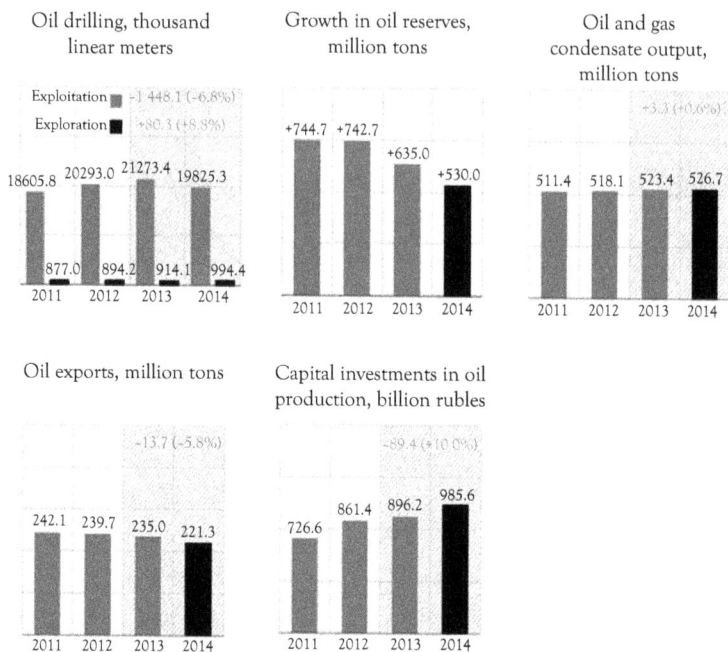

Figure 3.3 **Indicators for the Russian oil industry in 2014**

Source: Итоги работы Минэнерго России (2015).

Russia's dominant regional geoposition in gas exports; and a changing energy demand landscape where non-OECD economies (notably China and India) will account for the largest share of future fossil fuel demand. Similarly, the Russian Ministry of Energy envisions four major strategic challenges for the national energy sector: the growing competition and globalization of energy markets (shale gas, liquefied natural gas [LNG], and proliferation of spot prices, renewable energy) erodes Russia's market position; the global energy demand shifting from Europe (economic stagnation, diversification of energy imports, tightening regulations in ecology and energy efficiency) toward emerging economies (Asian-Pacific region, BRICs) necessitates a restructuring in the energy distribution system and the infrastructure; the worsening of the geopolitical situation, sanctions against the Russian energy sector create constraints in its access to critical state-of the art technologies/equipment, and potentially to global markets; and an abrupt drop of global prices on carbon energy and their uncertain future dynamics (Итоги работы Минэнерго России 2015).

Natural and associated petroleum gas output, billion cubic meters

−27.9 (−4.2%)

670.7   654.5   668.2   640.3

2011   2012   2013   2014

Domestic supply of natural gas, including liquefied associated gas, billion cubic meters

−2.3 (−0.5%)

469.1   460.0   456.9   454.6

2011   2012   2013   2014

Exports of natural gas, including liquefied associated gas, billion cubic meters

−22.1 (−10.9%)

196.8   186.2   203.3   181.2

2011   2012   2013   2014

Natural gas consumption as motor fuel, million cubic meters

+10 (+2.5%)

362   390   400   410

2011   2012   2013   2014

Capital investments in the gasification of the Russian economy, billion rubles

−5.1 (−15.0%)

29.0   33.7   33.9   28.8

2011   2012   2013   2014

Level of gasification of the Russian economy, percent

63.1   63.2   64.4   65.3

2011   2012   2013   2014

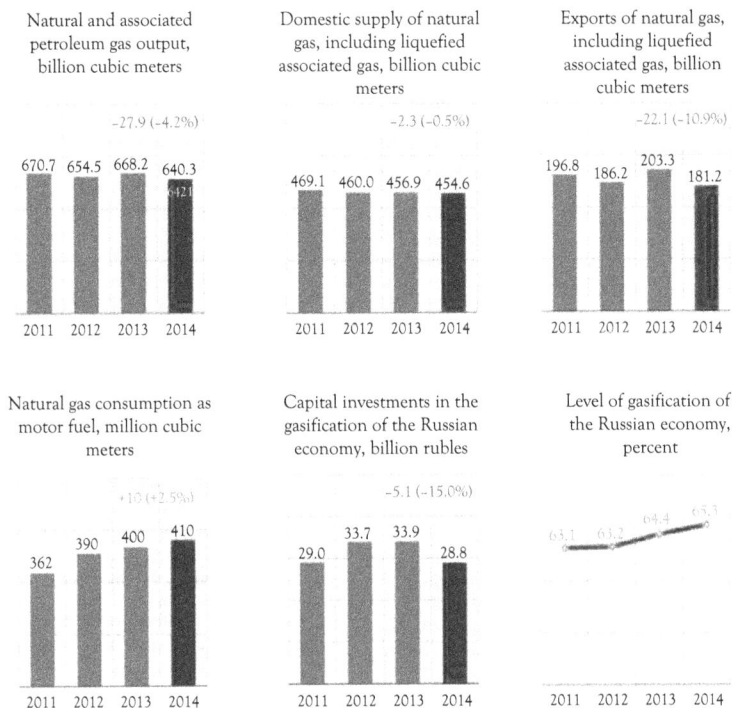

Figure 3.4 Indicators for the Russian natural gas industry in 2014

Source: Итоги работы Минэнерго России (2015).

Under these trends it remains to be seen whether Russia can lead a changing global market structure or whether it merely trails along. While the country could be at the helm of an OPEC-style organization to regulate gas supplies and prices, for example, it could also lose out to strong competition in the growing LNG sector and elsewhere. While Russia would be affected by global evolutions, changes in its surrounding regional energy environment may have greater impacts on its future. Russia has limited year-round maritime access, and is not a major global LNG exporter, its plans for expansion notwithstanding. Geographically, it is placed at the intersection of European and Asian markets. This location positions the country as a regional player, sensitive to developments that could affect its access to surrounding markets. Such developments might include the completion of future pipelines to bypass Russian, currently near monopolistic supply routes to Europe, a rise in alternative Mediterranean sources of energy, an increase in European LNG infrastructure, or changes in national and regional policies and regulatory environment (World Economic Forum 2013).

One formidable force revolutionizing the global energy landscape and reshaping Russia's place and role in it is shale oil and gas exploitation that has spiked over the past few years. Owing to relatively recent technological advances (more details in Orr 2013), the United States is already competing with Russia in natural gas production and global supply. Its production prices are comparatively lower—according to the latest BP report, in 2014 average natural gas prices in some global regions ranged, in U.S. dollars per million Btu, from $16.33 for LNG Japan, to $9.11 for average import price in Germany, to $4.35 for U.S. Henry, to $3.87 for Alberta, Canada (BP Statistical Review of World Energy 2015). Under these dynamics there are prospects for the United States to become a major LNG exporter in the years to come, possibly profoundly changing the global gas landscape. Besides the gas itself, the United States has broad vested national and foreign policy interests in overcoming its own national dependence on energy imports and nonenergy policy priorities. This translates into government action. Before long, U.S. experience, if proved positive, will be replicated by Europe, Russia's major customer in energy supply, and by China, Russia's important potential energy market. In this context, "it is surprising how little Russia seems to take into account the threat shale gas represents to its core energy edge" (World Economic Forum 2013). Methane hydrates, a product resulting from new emerging technology, is another potential disruptive innovation in unconventional energy.[4] If successful on a large scale, it may further erode Russia's global leadership in exports and, with the nation's continuous massive dependence on energy exports, undermine domestic growth and political-economic stability. Yet another challenge to Russia's energy-based

---

[4] Methane hydrates are natural gas molecules trapped in ice that may offer a potentially abundant source of natural gas widely distributed across the globe. Assuming the extraction technology can be mastered, methane hydrates could offer traditionally resource-poor countries greater energy security. While shale gas developments are already causing fundamental changes in the global energy sector, shale gas deposits as a proportion of global natural gas supplies may seem minor in comparison to methane hydrates (Methane Hydrates 2013; International Gas Hydrate Research 2014).

global strategic edge may be presented by the worldwide proliferation of policies and solutions toward sustainability, efficiency, and the emerging global transition toward low-carbon economies. Although fossil fuels are likely to remain dominant in the global energy consumption mix, several nonoil and gas supplies (e.g., coal and its derivatives) could at least partially meet global energy demand. Additional factors include the advent of carbon capture and storage, nuclear power, proliferation of renewable energies, and other disruptive innovations translated into new political-economic paradigms in energy. In many ways, these dynamics may turn detrimental for Russia and ultimately diminish its global strategic superiority grounded in oil and gas. While Russia could make further use of its coal, nuclear, and hydropower resources, its economy remains dependent on a highly energy-intensive and fossil fuel-driven growth model—which is clearly in transition. For long-term sustainability, Russia needs to explore ways in which it can benefit from a global transition toward low-carbon growth (World Economic Forum 2013).

Dynamics in the Domestic Energy Sector

Further discussion shifts to production, distribution, consumption, logistics, and efficiency in the Russian energy sector, specifically in fossil fuels—Russia's strategically most important segment. As noted earlier, Russia holds top global positions in proved reserves, production, and consumption for the fossils (Table 3.3). These positions are particularly strong in oil and natural gas where Russia also maintains superb rankings, respectable market shares in global exports, and enjoys strategic superiority ingrained in energy dependency on the part of the consuming countries whose alternatives to Russian fossils are limited.

Oil Industry: Reserves, Production, Consumption, and Exports

At the end of 2015, Russia's proven oil reserves were 102.4 billion barrels (bbl.)[5] or 6.0 percent of the world's total (BP Statistical Review of

---

[5] World Economic Outlook 2012's estimate of Russian proved oil reserves is approximately 120 billion barrels (World Energy Outlook, 2012, 98).

Table 3.3 Russia's energy sector: Proved reserves, production, consumption, and role in the world, at the end of 2015

Proved reserves			Production			Consumption		
World rank	Volume	Share of total, percent	World rank	Volume	Share of total, percent	World rank	Volume	Share of total, percent
Oil								
6	102.4[1]	6.0	3	10,980[2]	12.4	6	3,113[2]	3.3
Natural gas								
2	32,300[3]	17.3	2	573.3[3]	16.1	2	391.5[3]	11.2
Coal								
2	157,010[4]	17.6	6	184.5[5]	4.8	6	88.7[5]	2.3
Nuclear energy								
NA	NA	NA	NA	NA	NA	3	44.2[5]	7.6
Hydroelectricity								
NA	NA	NA	NA	NA	NA	5	38.5[5]	4.3
Renewable energy								
NA	NA	NA	NA	NA	NA	Low	0.1[5]	<0.05

Source: Compiled from BP Statistical Review of World Energy, June (2016).
Note: [1]Thousand million barrels.
[2]Thousand barrels daily.
[3]Billion cubic meters.
[4]Million tons.
[5]Million tons oil equivalent.

World Energy 2016). Most of Russia's proven oil resources are located in Western Siberia and in the Volga-Urals region, extending south into the Caspian Sea—far from Russia's major energy-consuming industrial clusters nationwide and even farther yet from energy markets worldwide.[6] Eastern Siberia holds some reserves, but the region, characterized by

---

[6] Putting Russian geography in perspective, it takes more than 6 days for a passenger train to cover the distance of 9,289 km (5,771 miles) between Moscow and Vladivostok and cross 7 time zones over the Trans-Siberian Railway. Freight trains are much slower. There are very limited cost-efficient logistical alternatives to freight trains since Russia has only three-year-round warm water ports (Murmansk, Novorossiysk and Vladivostok—all of them are extremely disjoined from each other geographically) plus access to some minor ports in the Baltic Sea that freeze in winter.

difficult terrain, harsh climate conditions, and underdeveloped socioeconomic infrastructure, has had little exploration. As shown in Figure 3.5, in 2014, Russia produced an estimated 10.8 million barrels per day (bbl/d) of total liquids (of which 93 percent was crude oil), and consumed roughly 3.2 million bbl/d (BP Statistical Review of World Energy 2015; Russia: Country Profile 2015).

Although several new oil exploration projects are in development, these projects at best may only be able to offset declining output from aging fields and not generate significant output growth in the near-term (more analytical specifics can be obtained from Итоги работы Минэнерго России 2015). The use of more advanced technologies and the application of improved recovery techniques result in increased oil output from existing oil deposits. Russia has 40 oil refineries with a total crude oil processing capacity of 5.5 million bbl/d. Rosneft, the largest refinery operator, controls 1.3 million bbl/d and operates Russia's largest refinery, the 385,176-bbl/d Angarsk facility in southern part of the lake Baikal, an ecologically sensitive area. Other companies with sizeable refining capacity in Russia include LUKoil (975,860 bbl/d) and TNK-BP[7] (690,000 bbl/d) (U.S. Energy Information Administration 2015). Additional specifics on the oil industry can be obtained from the annual report "Итоги работы Минэнерго России" (2015) by the Russian Ministry of Energy (Table 3.4).

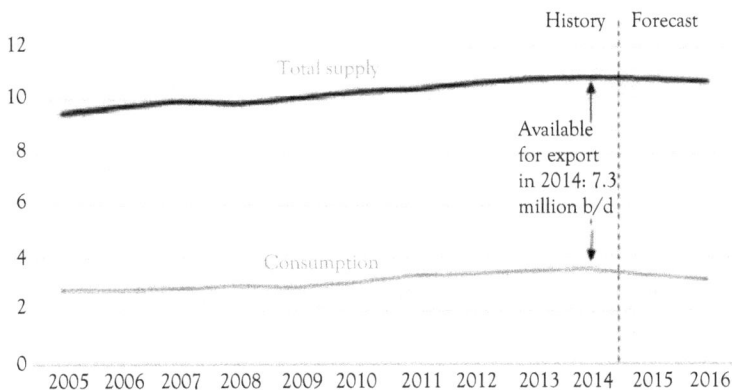

Figure 3.5 Russia's oil production, consumption, and availability for export, 2005–2016

Source: U.S. Department of Energy (2015).

---

[7] In 2013 TNK-BP was acquired by Russian-based company Rosneft.

Table 3.4 Russia: Oil production by regions, 2013

Region	Thousand bbl/d
Western Siberia	6,422
Urals-Volga	2,310
Krasnoyarsk	426
Sakhalin	277
Arkhangelsk	269
Komi Republic	257
Irkutsk	227
Yakutia	149
North Caucasus	62
Kaliningrad	26
Total	10,435

Source: U.S. Energy Information Administration (2015).

Natural Gas Industry: Reserves, Production, Consumption, and Exports

As of January 1, 2015, Russia held the world's largest natural gas reserves, with 1,688 trillion cubic feet (Tcf). Russia's reserves account for about a quarter of the world's total proven reserves. The majority of these reserves are remotely located in Siberia, with the Yamburg, Urengoy, and Medvezh'ye fields alone accounting for more than 40 percent of Russia's total reserves, while other significant deposits are located in northern Russia.

The state-run Gazprom dominates Russia's upstream, producing about 74 percent of Russia's total natural gas output. Gazprom also controls most of Russia's gas reserves, with more than 65 percent of proven reserves being directly controlled by the company and additional reserves being controlled by Gazprom in joint ventures with other companies.

While independent producers have gained importance, with producers such as Novatek and LUKoil contributing increasing volumes to Russia's production in recent years, upstream opportunities remain fairly limited for independent producers and other companies, including Russian oil majors. Gazprom's position is further cemented by its legal monopoly on Russian gas exports, although that may be ending soon. Russia's government has announced its intent to liberalize LNG exports starting January 2014, breaking Gazprom's absolute export monopoly

(U.S. Energy Information Administration 2015). In Russia, natural gas associated with oil production is often flared. Russia flared an estimated 1,320 Bcf (billion cubic feet) of natural gas in 2011—more than any other country. At this level, Russia alone accounted for about a stunning 27 percent of the total volume of gas flared globally in 2011. Although a number of Russian government initiatives and policies have set reduction targets for gas flaring, decreases have not yet occurred. Government efforts to decrease the widespread practice of gas flaring and enforce gas utilization requirements for oil extraction may result in additional increases in production. Russia sends about 90 percent of its natural gas exports to customers in Europe, with Germany, Turkey, Italy, France, and the United Kingdom receiving the bulk of these volumes. Smaller volumes of natural gas are also shipped via the Gazprom pipeline network to Austria, Finland, and Greece. Russia is also an exporter of LNG. The Sakhalin Energy's LNG plant has been operating since 2009 and can export up to 788 MMcf (million cubic feet) of LNG per year on two trains. The majority of the LNG has been contracted to Japanese and South Korean buyers under long-term supply agreements. In 2014, Sakhalin LNG exports went to Japan (79 percent), South Korea (18 percent), China (1 percent), Taiwan (1 percent), and Thailand (1 percent). There are other proposals in various stages of planning and construction for new LNG terminals in Russia, including Yamal LNG and Shtokman LNG (this project is currently stalled and is highly uncertain) (U.S. Energy Information Administration 2015). Additional specifics on the natural gas industry can be obtained from the annual report "Итоги работы Минэнерго России" (2015) by the Russian Ministry of Energy.

Sectors of the Russian Economy Attractive from International Business Perspective

As argued earlier in chapter 1, in a broad sense, a country's attractiveness in the international business perspective varies, depending on whether the overseas expansion is export-driven or manufacturing-driven. This attractiveness can be generally rationalized in terms of strategic benefits, costs, and risks, as well as other priorities in the company, industry, and country analytical context. As an illustration of Russia's market attractiveness and analytical approach in rationalizing an international market decision, we use the Doing Business in Russia (2016) report by the U.S. Commercial Service. Information from this includes three selected examples reflecting best marketing opportunities for American companies in Russia: Agricultural Equipment, Medical Equipment, and Cosmetics and Perfumery. In contrast to the previous discussion of the Russian energy sector covering general scope, drivers, dynamics, and trends, the Doing Business in Russia (2016) report has commercial, marketing emphasis. Additionally, and beyond specific marketing information, these three examples provide useful analytical tools and frameworks to aid in decision making for strategic expansion to Russia.

Best Prospect: Agricultural Equipment

Overview

Russia contains 220 million hectares or 20 percent of the world's supply of fertile land and according to Food and Agriculture Organization of the United Nations (FAO) could potentially feed 2 billion people, but this potential is not fully developed yet. General information characterizing Russian market for agricultural equipment is presented in Table 3.5.

The increasing need for modernized agricultural machinery in Russia is clear. Inadequate agricultural machinery and equipment still remains the weakness of Russian agricultural production. In the last 10 years, the fleet of tractors decreased 40 percent, with similar large reductions in the number of plows (55 percent), seeders (52 percent), grain harvesters (50 percent), and forage harvesters (49 percent). Almost 50 percent of harvesters owned by Russian farmers exceed the normal service age of 10 to 12 years. In Russia, one tractor serves 247 hectares, compared to

Table 3.5 Agricultural equipment in Russia, $U.S. thousand

	2010	2011	2012	2013	2014
Total market size	1,700,000	4,066,000	4,675,900	4,366,600	n/a
Total local production	833,000	1,339,000	1,236,000	n/a	n/a
Total exports	176,620	130,170	96,000	180,000	73,000
Total imports	1,044,000	2,857,000	3,514,100	2,576,000	1,706,500

Sources: Estimates from Russian Association of Agricultural Machinery Producers.

38 hectares in the United States and 14 in France. Market players and experts have consistently expressed the view that there is a significant need for a large-scale replacement of old agricultural equipment in the next few years.

Farmers' finances have been slowly recovering from the 2010 drought and the low crop prices in the beginning of 2011. However, their indebtedness, worsening economic conditions, and increased prices for agricultural inputs limit their ability to purchase new equipment. In February 2015, the Russian government introduced a grain export tariff, (minimum 35 Euros per ton) until June 30, 2015, with the aim to stabilize prices for bread and flour and prevent high volumes of grain exports. On May 15, 2015, the export fee was temporarily revoked. A new nominal export fee of minimum 50 Rub per ton (approximately $1) is effective from July 1, 2015.

The general deterioration in economic conditions and uncertainty in the market place coupled with increased interest rates, unstable exchange rates, and delayed government support dampened demand for large capital purchases and slowed investment. While there was an increase in imports of certain types of equipment, such as tractors, cultivators, and forage harvesters, the overall market dropped in 2014. According to Russian customs statistics, imports of machines and equipment in 2014 decreased by 8.7 percent. According to the Association of Agricultural Equipment Producers "Rosagromash," the Russian agricultural equipment market shrank by 3.8 percent in 2014.

Leading Russian producers of agricultural equipment are Rostselmash, St. Petersburg Tractor Plant, and Klever Company (OOO "Klever").

Leading foreign producers of agricultural equipment (with varying levels of local content) are John Deere (USA), CNH (USA), Claas (Germany), and AGCO (USA).

- Although there is growth potential in Russia for agricultural equipment in the long-run, there are several serious challenges confronting the agricultural sector at the moment: High interest rates for purchasing agricultural equipment (current interest rates from Rosselkhozbank and Sberbank vary from 18 to 23 percent).

- Reduction in government subsidies for agricultural producers coupled with rapid price growth for raw materials and energy.
- Low growth in foreign investments in the sector.
- Unstable demand for agricultural equipment, due to financial instability of Russian farming enterprises.

There is little optimism for agricultural equipment market development to trend positively. The current economic and political situation presents certain challenges to developing a strong market for foreign products. In general, experts suggest that the agricultural equipment market in 2015 will be two or three times less than in 2014. The factors mentioned previously decrease demand for new agricultural equipment and force agricultural producers to delay capital investment or look for cheaper options and, at least in the short term, switch to local agricultural equipment producers.

Subsector Best Prospects

Cultivators and other soil preparation equipment include plows, harrows, cultivators, seeders, and fertilizer spreaders; equipment for dairy livestock breeding, swine, and poultry production; milk processing and animal feed preparation equipment.

Opportunities

The agricultural sector, like the rest of the Russian economy, experienced a downturn in 2014 and 2015, but it still requires substantial investment to ensure that it is equipped to provide food security. In the long term, it is important to stay connected with the market and use every window of opportunity to remain active in the market. At the same time, the Russian government has made it a priority to ensure food security for the nation by increasing the amount of agricultural products produced in Russia. Therefore, there is a demand for agricultural equipment that allows increasing yield and labor capacity as well as guaranteeing ecological safety and a safe work environment. The Russian government plans significant investments in projects that will help substitute import of meat, milk, and vegetables over the next five years. The Ministry of Agriculture endorsed 464 projects for the total of 263 billion rubles (approximately 5 billion USD that will receive government support. In 2015, the Russia government developed a program to compensate up to 30 percent of the direct construction cost of milk plants.

U.S. firms interested in the Russian agricultural machinery market should consider exhibiting at one of the key Russian agricultural trade shows. These trade shows are a powerful marketing tool and reassure Russian buyers that the American supplier is committed to establishing and maintaining its presence in the Russian market. Sales are often made at these trade events. U.S. companies may also find opportunities when financially healthy Russian companies are seeking to expand in order to satisfy a growing demand for domestically produced food. For example, there may be opportunities to sell meat, fruit, and vegetable processing equipment due to increased sales in these segments.

Best Prospect: Russia—Cosmetics and Perfumery

Overview

General information characterizing Russian market of for cosmetics and perfumery is presented in Table 3.6. Data Sources: Total Local Production: www.rbc.ru; Total Exports: Global Trade Atlas; Total Imports: Global Trade Atlas; Imports from United States: Global Trade Atlas. Industry experts convey that the beauty sector (cosmetics, nutraceuticals, and beauty treatments) has proven to be recession-proof, and fortunately, such a situation is unfolding in the wake of a recession in Russia. Russian

Table 3.6 Russia cosmetics and perfumery market size, USD, thousand

	2013	2014	2015 (est.)	2016 (est.)
Total market size	10,330,000	10,362,860	n/a	n/a
Total local production	6,950,000	7,260,000	n/a	n/a
Total exports	377,000	520,000	n/a	n/a
Total imports	3,757,000	3,622,000	n/a	n/a
Imports from the United States	253,511	280,027	n/a	n/a
Exchange rate: 1 USD	31.9	38.69	n/a	n/a

Total Market Size = (Total Local Production + Total Imports) − (Total Exports).

attitudes toward cosmetics and their curiosity for new products and technologies have translated into a lucrative market that rewards foreign companies that invest their time and resources. Despite the slowdown in the Russian economy, Russian distributors and retailers have remained bullish in launching new brands and product lines to sustain demand. Since 2014, American brands such as Living Proof, Patchology, Revitalash, Unwash, Kevin Murphy, V76, and R + Co have entered the Russian market and established successful partnerships with Russian distribution companies. Even Russia's largest retail chain of beauty shops L'etoile (900 shops), which carries many U.S. brands, plans to open another 100 new stores this year. As of April 2015, leading analytical companies are not ready to provide reports on the market of cosmetics and perfumery in Russia for 2014; currently they are making recalculations in connection with changing exchange rates at the end of 2014. With forecasts for the current year, experts are in no hurry as well; analysts do not dare to predict the level of reduction in customer demand so far, preferring to draw first conclusions after the ruble stabilizes.

In 2014, the following countries were the leading suppliers (by value) to Russia: France (29 percent), Poland (10 percent), Italy (10 percent), United States (9 percent), and Italy (9 percent). Table 3.7 provides information on imports of cosmetic products.

The following trends can be highlighted in the current market of cosmetics in Russia: The cosmetologist remains an important link for professional cosmetics; growing interest toward the South-East and Asian cosmetics manufacturers; increasing sales of home care products in beauty salons; women switching to a slightly less expensive brand still within the

Table 3.7 The share of imports of cosmetic products by types in 2014

Type of product	Percent
Lips makeup	11
Eye makeup	15
Products for manicure and pedicure	7
Powder (including compact)	5
Other cosmetics or makeup	62
Total	100

Source: Federal Customs Service, I-Marketing agency.

premium segment; development of beauty salon chains; increasing sales of professional cosmetics via Internet.

The main segments of the market are the following: perfumes (23 percent), skin care products (22.6 percent), hair care (19.2 percent), and makeup (15.4 percent). A large number of international companies already have a strong presence in the Russian beauty market. Multinational companies such as L'Oreal, Beiersdorf, and Unilever are market leaders.

Domestic manufacturers hold the lion's share of the market. Major Russian manufacturers include Kalina, Nevskaya Kosmetika, Svoboda, Vesna, Arnest, Alfa Kosmeca, Faberlic, Mezoplast, and Unikosmetik. The competition between foreign and local manufacturers in the mass-market and middle-market segments is strong. Generally, foreign producers outpace local producers in the use of new technologies with respect to manufacturing processes and larger marketing and advertising budgets. Contract manufacturing is growing in popularity in Russia, because companies are trying to significantly reduce their costs. These companies include wholesalers, specialized retail chains, pharmacies, and larger manufacturers such as Kalina and Nevskaya Kosmetica. About 90 percent of all domestic brands specialize in face and body products. The situation is more complicated with decorative cosmetics since there is only one domestic makeup manufacturer, Art-Visage factory. The Russian company produces approximately 35 million products of decorative cosmetics per year, which is 95 percent of all color cosmetics produced in the market.

Skin care: A slowdown in income growth has impacted consumers of skincare products. Industry experts state that consumer choices have become more and more selective. In most cases they are willing to pay for effective solutions, but are on the lookout for special prices and discounts. Russians always seek value (i.e., high quality and lower prices) for their solutions. Mass market skin care manufacturers are successful in attracting consumers with new product developments, more convenience, and eye-catching packaging.

Hair care: Professional salon hair care and premium hair care products have strong demand in Russia. Industry insiders convey that novelties and professional positioning are the main drivers in this particular segment in

Russia. Russians place a high premium on natural products. Therefore, brands that include remedies perform better on the market, especially hair loss treatments and medicated shampoos. Salon hair care is one of the healthiest subsectors within the hair care segment.

Oral care: Market contacts express that interest in innovative oral care pushes demand for professional products in Russia. Russians perception of oral care goes beyond regular toothpaste and toothbrushes. There is a strong interest in additional oral care products such as rinses, threads, and gum balms. Market players have expanded the range of well-known brands with specially developed professional lines. Russian consumers care about their appearance, which has positively impacted sales of oral care products.

Children's skin care: The number of children aged 0 to 14 is increasing in Russia. This forms a positive basis for growth of baby and child-care cosmetic products. Russian parents are becoming more educated about local and international brands and have become more selective. Their preference is for high-quality products that are safe for children.

Color cosmetics: Russians actively seek premium products since they are perceived as being of higher quality. Novelties continue to be the main development tool for color cosmetics in Russia. Professional positioning positively impacts mass-market and premium-class cosmetics products. Russian consumers look for the most effective ways to enhance their looks. Branded, high-value products have developed much faster, especially in the major cities where they are associated with a higher social status.

Professional cosmetics: Industry insiders believe that the modern market of professional cosmetics is a promising one, showing positive growth trends. According to the research group Step-by-Step, professional cosmetics account for 12 to 13 percent of the total cosmetics market in Russia in monetary terms, and in the next few years experts expect gradual growth of this particular segment. Professional products for face and body, anti-age, and anticellulite treatment are most in demand, particularly various peeling systems and instant lifting cosmetics with a Botox-like effect are very popular. There is a noticeable focus toward products with visible impacts. People seeking slimming and antiaging treatments are becoming frequent visitors at salons.

Despite the fact that the market is close to saturation, growth points are still available, especially in Russia's regions. Regional markets are growing but at a lower rate since the current economic downturn. The regional markets of Kazan and Yekaterinburg are smaller in terms of capacity, but they are less saturated and more receptive to new products. Regional consumers are more easily attracted by various promotion events, ads, and articles in mass media. The cosmetics market recently experienced significant changes to the distribution network with retailers becoming the key players replacing distributors. According to RBK Research Agency, cosmetics and toiletries distribution channels include: cosmetic retail chains (33.5 percent); other (supermarkets, Internet) (32.1 percent); direct sales (21.9 percent); outdoor markets (7.2 percent); and pharmacies (5.3 percent).

Since the beginning of 2014, there was a downturn of 25 percent in the number of consumers going to beauty shops. The assortment of products offered in retail chains has also changed with middle-market and mass-market brands complementing exclusive in-house products. The share of mass-market products in retail chains has grown to 30 percent in the last few years. An additional channel for mass-market and middle-market brands, as well as for cosmeceuticals, is pharmacy chains. Russian consumers perceive cosmetics sold through pharmacies to be more reputable, safer, and effective. General managers of large beauty shop chains estimate that at the price of imported cosmetics increased from 20 to 50 percent in the first half of 2015. Russian producers also raised prices on products, from 10 to 15 percent, and could raise them further because domestic cosmetics are made of around 80 percent of imported raw materials (main suppliers are the United States and Asia).

The new list of cosmetic products that are subject to the declaration of conformity and state registration in Russia, Kazakhstan, and Belarus (members of the Eurasian Economic Commission) went into force on September 25, 2014. Decision No. 145 of the Eurasian Economic Commission Collegiate of 25 August 2014 amends the List of Cosmetic Products for which a customs declaration must be submitted together with a conformity assessment document (i.e., a state registration certificate or a declaration of conformity). The conformity assessment document verifies that the products comply with the Customs Union Technical Regulation on Cosmetics and Perfumery TR CU 009/2011.

The new amendments increase the maximum hydrogen peroxide concentration limit, from 0.6 to 6.0 percent (included or released) in tooth bleaching products for which state registration is required (rather than a declaration of conformity). This means that a wider range of tooth whitening products will be subject to the state registration procedure. In addition, state registration becomes mandatory for cosmetic products manufactured with the use of nanomaterials.

Subsector Best Prospects

The segment of antiaging products remains the main category for expansion and further development in Russia. Also, experts predict growth in the share of the organic cosmetics segment in Russia. The best sales prospects include the following categories: antiaging and body care professional equipment, affordable color cosmetics, skin and hair care products from mass-high to high-end, professional skin and hair care products for beauty salons, manicure and pedicure products, cosmetics for children, and niche perfumery.

Opportunities

Perfumes, skin care, hair care, and decorative cosmetics are most the prominent product categories in the Russian cosmetics market. The highest demand is in the professional market segment. Distributors seek unique, state-of-the-art technologies that could be offered to doctors and professional estheticians. Russian consumers traditionally trust foreign brands more than local ones due to their consistency of quality and product reputation, as market experts' state. According to industry specialists, the future of the Russian cosmetics and toiletries market is in niche marketing and narrow customization. Given the intense competition between foreign and local manufacturers, especially in the mass-market and middle-market segments, the cost of entering and developing the market is much higher than in previous years. In the near future, success will largely be dependent on significant investments in advertising, marketing and promotion, and participation and promotion at specialized trade shows. U.S. manufacturers can improve their market visibility by offering exclusive cosmetic products and by employing qualified agents/distributors in the market. Price continues to be the most competitive factor, which could limit export opportunities. U.S. producers could consider opening a representative office to initiate and strengthen agreements with retailers and other potential importers.

Web Resources

Organizations: Association of Manufacturers of Perfumery, Cosmetics, Household, and Hygiene goods www.apcohm.org; Russian Association of Perfumery and Cosmetics www.pcar.ru; Spa and Wellness International Council www.1swic.ru; Society of Aesthetic Medicine of Russia www.rs-am.ru.

Consumer Trends, Middle Class, and Marketing Strategies

There is widespread and growing awareness of the strategic importance of emerging markets. Currently, more than 20,000 multinationals are operating in emerging economies; according to the Economist, Western multinationals expect to find 70 percent of their future growth there—40 percent of it in China and India alone. Eyring, Johnson, and Hari (2011) developed a business framework facilitating innovation and implementation process for emerging markets. At its most basic level, the process consists of three steps: identify an important unmet job a target customer needs done; blueprint a model that can accomplish that job profitably for a price the customer is willing to pay; and carefully implement and evolve the model by testing essential assumptions and adjusting as the business learns. According to the framework, there are three core consumer product and service segments in emerging markets: expensive high-end products and services, targeting the very few who can afford them, cheap low-end products, and services targeting the masses enjoying very limited purchasing power. Between these two extremes, there is a promising vast middle market. Consumers there are defined not so much by any particular income band as by a common circumstance; their needs are being met very poorly by existing low-end solutions because they cannot afford even the cheapest of the high-end alternatives. Companies that devise new business models and offerings to better meet those consumers' needs affordably will discover enormous opportunities for growth. Put in other words, there is a sizeable and growing middle class that can afford more sophisticated products under the right marketing mix, the 4Ps.

According to Nielsen, a consultancy, stable gross domestic product growth, declining inflation, and a record-low unemployment rate are pointing to positive consumer purchasing power in Russia. The Russian middle class, which stands at 104 million strong, is fueling that power. This segment of the population is projected to rise 16 percent between now and 2020, at which point it will represent 86 percent of the population and amount to $1.3 trillion in spending—up 40 percent from 2010, based on a global study of the emerging middle class and related databases by the Brookings Institution. "There is an equal share of money at the top and in the middle," said Dr. Venkatesh Bala, chief economist, the Cambridge Group, a part of Nielsen, "Russia's middle class today has the same share of income as the upper class and has remained an untapped opportunity by many international corporations." Although the top 20 percent of income earners in Russia represent 47 percent of the country's total income, the middle 60 percent accounts for 48 percent, according to federal statistics from the Bank of Russia (2012). The bottom 20 percent comprise the remaining 5 percent of income.

While many companies have focused on Russia's central and northwest districts—where Moscow and St. Petersburg are located and the wealth is more concentrated—the south, Volga and Ural districts have an almost equal share of income and are growing at faster rates. Marketers will need to take initiative in order to grow Russian consumption. Retail trade turnover has slowed from double-digit year-over-year growth in 2008 (14 percent) to single-digit growth in 2012 (6 percent). Furthermore, household consumption remains low (49 percent of GDP) compared with other countries, and has fallen from 54 percent since 1996–1997, based on data from the Bank of Russia and Cambridge Group analysis. Russia's 53.2 percent share of household consumption in the GDP compares with 38.1 percent in China, 59.7 percent in India, 63.2 percent in Brazil, 68.8 percent in the United States, and 57 percent in the world overall (The World Factbook 2016). Consumption growth in Russia will come from two main sources: the growing middle-income consumer base and an expanded regional retail distribution network. A deep understanding of middle-class consumer segments will be necessary to deliver a strong portfolio of products that provide the benefits consumers want at the right price. Developing meaningful innovation and offering trade-up strategies will appeal to consumers' existing and aspirational needs and desires.

On the distribution front, Russia's retail landscape is fragmented, and the sheer size of the country makes logistical efficiency a challenge. Overcoming operational challenges, logistics and resource allocation in order to expand distribution outside the main cities will be vital to reaching the millions of consumers that represent untapped demand potential (A Rising Middle Class Will Fuel Growth in Russia 2013).

Euromonitor International (a.k.a. Passport and GMID), a global market research company, offers a wide array of market information on many countries, including Russia. Their flagship Consumer Lifestyles in Russia (Country Report: Russia 2016) report covers key marketing topics including: consumer trends, consumer segmentation, housing and households, money and savings, eating and drinking, grooming and fashion, health and wellness, shopping habits, leisure and recreation, and getting around (transport). The top five consumer trends in Russia identified by the report are as follows: consumer confidence low as a result of economic downturn; online shopping boosted by consumers looking for lower prices; Russians increasingly adopting healthier lifestyles; older Russians delaying retirement; and high cost of mortgages keeps many off the property ladder. Major findings characterizing these five trends are summarized as follows.

Consumer Confidence Low As a Result of Economic Downturn

Consumers have had to face numerous personal challenges as a result of the recent economic downturn brought about by declining oil prices, economic sanctions imposed by the West, and the devaluation of the ruble, among other factors. In addition, traditionally high rates of income inequality have made adjusting to the new economic reality more difficult.

Between 2013 and 2014, growth of both annual disposable income and consumer spending per household slowed significantly in real terms and then both declined in 2015 by a projected 10 percent, reaching RUB 683,347 and RUB 586,760, respectively. In particular, rising food prices are squeezing household budgets. As a result, consumers have postponed (or cancelled) shopping for discretionary goods. A recent article in the New York Times noted:

> The brand-new Avia Park is a glittering testament to the power of the Russian consumer. A panorama of white tile flooring, under a soaring, six story-tall glass roof, it is the largest mall in Europe. There is just one problem: It is a ghost town. Row after row, store-fronts are vacant. On a recent evening, a handful of visitors meandered past shops that have opened, but purchases are relatively rare. With no customers to serve, a chef at a Sbarro restaurant passed the time honing a knife.

Nevertheless, some observers see light at the end of the tunnel, speculating that the Russian economy has hit rock bottom and can only improve. In a recent article in the *Moscow Times*, Oleg Kuzmin, vice president at Renaissance Capital investment bank, said: "The main positive development is that, [in 2015], despite the economic downturn, the economy has remained sustainable, which will lead to an overall stabilization next year." Anton Struchenevsky, a senior economist at Sberbank CIB, was even more optimistic, noting:

> The economy has rather successfully adapted to new conditions caused by lower oil prices and problems with refinancing foreign debts ... What is most important is that there is no longer a feeling of panic ... The decline seems to be over.

Online Shopping Boosted by Consumers Looking for Lower Prices

As a result of the devaluation of the ruble and high inflation, a growing number of consumers have begun to shop online to purchase goods—including clothing, footwear, and electronics—that are now prohibitively expensive in brick-and-mortar stores. In addition to shopping on well-known international websites such as Amazon and eBay, consumers are increasingly looking to Chinese sites. Of course, Internet retailing was growing prior to the economic downturn. And for many shoppers it's not only about price. In numerous surveys, respondents have cited convenience and the wider selection of quality products as attractions of Internet retail sites. Improved payment and delivery systems have increased demand, as well. In addition to international sites, consumers are turning to large domestic sites that offer affordable goods. For example, Ulmart.ru offers an affordable array of electronics, household goods, perfume, and automotive parts, while retailers such as Ozon.ru offer jewelery, clothing, and books. While value sales per household of Internet retailers declined slightly (in real terms) between 2014 and 2015, they nevertheless reached RUB 12,540 in 2015, up from RUB 10,703 in 2013.

Russians Increasingly Adopting Healthier Lifestyles

Following a long tradition of high smoking prevalence, a strong drinking culture and a high-fat, high-calorie cuisine, consumers are becoming increasingly aware of the benefits of healthier lifestyles. This has led to a growing number of Russians cutting back on or eschewing these habits. For example, in 2014 smoking prevalence reached 38.6 percent, down from 44 percent in 2009 while the volume consumption of alcoholic drinks declined by 18 percent between 2009 and 2014. Indeed, many are now proactively making efforts to get fit and maintain their fitness. For those who need additional help in addressing their health issues, the government has introduced a number of measures to curb smoking and drinking. Many consumers are also choosing to eat healthier foods, buying and consuming more organic produce and fresh juices and cutting out refined sugars and dairy products. On the other hand, despite these efforts many Russians are still struggling with weight issues, with 32 percent of the adult population classified as overweight and 27 percent classified as obese in 2014. Regardless, life expectancy continues to rise, reaching 71.3 years in 2014, up from 68.6 years in 2009.

Older Russians Delaying Retirement

For a range of reasons, more older Russians are choosing to continue working rather than to retire. In some cases, older workers feel forced to continue working in order to maintain their standards of living in an environment of economic uncertainty. Although the country currently has one of the lowest retirement ages in the world—60 years old for women and 65 years old for men—but the average monthly pension in 2015 was set at RUB 10,000 to RUB 12,000, according to the State Pension Fund. According to a recent report from the World Bank, 40 percent of men of retirement age continue to work while 33 percent of women of retirement age continue to work. Rising inflation has also convinced many to stay in work as long as possible. In a 2015 article in the *Moscow Times*, one Moscow resident said: "Everything is twice as expensive, both food and clothes." Many pensioners must also add in the high cost of medicine, which has risen considerably in the face of the economic crisis because most medicine is imported. At the same time, many older Russians simply enjoy working and do not want to quit. Throughout the 2000s employment opportunities were plentiful and more older people who wanted to work could easily do so.

High Cost of Mortgages Keeps Many off the Property Ladder

The mortgage boom that the country experienced throughout 2013 and into 2014 was cut short by the recession. With interest rates projected to continue to rise, many prospective home buyers, particularly younger consumers, will no longer be able to afford new mortgages. Indeed, the number of new mortgages was projected to decline by 46 percent in 2015. According to a 2015 article in the *Moscow Times*, "The availability of mortgage credit has diminished because of the worsening macroeconomic situation. Some market players have stopped giving credit or have set annual interest rates of 20 percent or more." In order to address the mortgage slump and to assist those that are finding it difficult to repay their current mortgages, the government introduced a new "anti-crisis" subsidies program in June 2015. Under the program, interest rates on all new loans will be capped at 13 percent. For those with existing mortgages, the situation has gone from bad to worse with tens of thousands facing possible eviction for unpaid mortgage debt, according to a recent article on website Meduza.io. Many have been unable to repay on their mortgages because banks have been unwilling to restructure current loans or they have imposed high interest rates in order to do so. The situation has affected housing demand, with more consumers turning to smaller and smaller spaces. In a 2015 article in Vedomosti, the head of the analytical real estate firm IRN said: "As money grows tighter, buyers are favoring smaller, cheaper apartments." Previously, prospective home buyers looked for two-bedroom apartments, but now demand has grown for studios and one-bedroom apartments. In addition, many young Russians find themselves out of the market altogether and many of them live with their extended families.

References

"BP Statistical Review of World Energy June 2016." www.bp.com/content/dam/bp/pdf/energy-economics/statistical-review-2016/bp-statistical-review-of-world-energy-2016-full-report.pdf (accessed September 18, 2016).

"Consumer Lifestyles in Russia." January 2016. "Euromonitor International (Passport)." www.euromonitor.com/consumer-lifestyles-in-russia/report

"Country Report: Russia." September 4, 2016. Economist Intelligence Unit, p. 11. http://country.eiu.com/russia

Curtis, G.E. ed. 1996. *Russia: A Country Study*. 1998. Washington, DC: GPO for the Library of Congress. http://lcweb2.loc.gov/frd/cs/rutoc.html

Deloitte. 2015. "Doing business in Russia 2015. Tax and Legal." www2.deloitte.com/content/dam/Deloitte/ru/Documents/tax/doing-business-in-Russia-2015.pdf

Eyring, MJ., M.W. Johnson, and H. Nair. January 2011. "New Business Models in Emerging Markets." *Harvard Business Review* 89, no. ½, pp. 88–95.

Federal State Statistics Service. 2015. *Russia' 2015 Statistical Pocketbook*. Moscow: Rosstat. www.gks.ru/free_doc/doc_2015/rus15_eng.pdf

globalEDGE. 2016. "Russia: Corporations." globalEDGE.msu.edu. http://globaledge.msu.edu/countries/russia/corporations

Global Entrepreneurship Monitor. 2016. "Russia: Country Profile." www.gemconsortium.org/country-profile/104

Index of Economic Freedom. 2016. Heritage Foundation. www.heritage.org/index/ranking.

International Energy Agency. 2015. "World Energy Outlook 2015."

Lawrence, P.R., and C. Vlachoutsicos. eds. 1990. *Behind the Factory Walls: Decision Making in Soviet and U.S. Enterprises.* Boston: Harvard Business School Press.

"Oil & Gas in Russia." December 2014. "MarketLine." Reference code: 0153-2116.

Orr, I. November 2013. "Hydraulic Fracturing: A Game-Changer for Energy and Economies." The Heartland Institute, Policy study No. 132—November 2013. www.heartland.org/_template-assets/documents/publications/11-10-13_isaac_orr_on_fracking.pdf

Retailing in Russia. July 2015. "Euromonitor International." www.euromonitor.com/retailing-in-russia/report

"A Rising Middle Class Will Fuel Growth in Russia." Nielsen.com. Last modified March 27, 2013. www.nielsen.com/us/en/insights/news/2013/a-rising-middle-class-will-fuel-growth-in-russia.html

Russia: Country Profile. 2016. "Passport/Euromonitor International." Russia. Country Report. 2015. Energy Information Administration. www.eia.gov/beta/international/analysis_includes/countries_long/Russia/russia.pdf

Russia' 2015 Statistical Pocketbook. 2015. "Federal State Statistics Service (Rosstat)." www.gks.ru/free_doc/doc_2015/rus15_eng.pdf

Schwab, K. 2015. *The Global Competitiveness Report 2015–2016.* Geneva: World Economic Forum. www3.weforum.org/docs/gcr/2015-2016/Global_Competitiveness_Report_2015-2016.pdf

"The World Factbook." Central Intelligence Agency. 2016. www.cia.gov/library/publications/the-world-factbook/.

U.S. Commercial Service. 2015a. *A Basic Guide to Exporting,* ed. Doug Barry. 11th ed. Washington DC: U.S. Department of Commerce. http://export.gov/basicguide/

U.S. Commercial Service. 2016. "Russia: Country Commercial Guide." Russia www.export.gov/article?id=Russia-openness-to-foreign-investment

U.S. Department of Energy. 2015. "Russia: International Energy and Data Analysis." Eia.gov. Last updated July 28, 2015.

U.S. Department of State. 2016. "Russia Investment Climate Statement 2016." www.state.gov/e/eb/rls/othr/ics/investmentclimatestatements/index.htm?year=2016&dlid=254409.

World Economic Forum. 2013. "Scenarios for the Russian Federation." www.weforum.org/reports/scenarios-russian-federation.

Zhuplev, A. 2014. "Russia: Ambitions and Ammunitions in Global Economic Competitiveness." In Geo-Regional Competitiveness in Central and Eastern Europe, the Baltic Countries, and Russia. ed. A. Zhuplev and K. Liuhto. Hershey: IGI Global.

Zhuplev, A., and D. Shtykhno. 2015. "Energy and Sustainability in the European Region: The Russian Factor." In Handbook of Research on Sustainable Development and Economics. ed. K.D. Thomas. Hershey: IGI Global.

Итоги работы Минэнерго России и основные результаты функционирования ТЭК в 2014 году: Задачи на среднесрочную перспективу (The Results and Performance of the Russian Energy Sector in 2014: Mid-range Goals and Outlook). 2015. Министр энергетики Российской Федерации А.В. Новак Москва, 15 апреля 2015 г. http://minenergo.gov.ru/upload/iblock/36e/prezentatsiya-itogovoy-kollegii.pdf.

Российская экономика в 2014 году. Тенденции и перспективы. (Выпуск 36). 2015. Издательство Института Гайдара. Москва. (Russian Economy in 2014. Trends and Outlooks. Issue 36. M.: Gaidar Institute Publishers. 576 pp.) http://iep.ru/files/text/trends/2014/Book.pdf.

Index